Demons
Defeated

Demons
Defeated

BILL SUBRITZKY

Sovereign World

Sovereign World Ltd
P.O. Box 17
Chichester PO20 6YB
England

International edition 1986
Reprinted 1987

© Copyright 1985 Dove Ministries Ltd
P.O. Box 48036
Blockhouse Bay, Auckland
New Zealand

All Scripture quotations are from the New King James Bible.

ISBN 1 85240 001 3

DEDICATION

To The Glory Of God

Other books from the same author:

Receiving the Gifts of the Holy Spirit
How to Receive the Baptism with the Holy Spirit
How to Know the Anointing of God
But I Don't Believe in Miracles!

The following are available in VHS video:

Deliverance from Demons (five hours)
Receiving the Gifts of the Holy Spirit (four hours)
The Bill Subritzky Story (one hour)
How to Receive the Baptism with the Holy Spirit
(one hour)

All enquiries write to:

Sovereign World Ltd.   OR   Dove Ministries
P.O. Box 17   P.O. Box 48036
Chichester PO20 6YB   Blockhouse Bay
England.   Auckland,
                                                       New Zealand.

Overseas Sovereign World Addresses

P.O. Box 329, Manly, N.S.W. 2095, Australia
P.O. Box 24086, Royal Oak, Auckland, New Zealand
14 Balmoral Road, Singapore 1025

CONTENTS

FOREWORD

This book has been written in order to encourage members of the Body of Christ to know their authority in Jesus Christ in order both to be set free themselves and to help set free others.

It has not been an easy book to write but I believe that it deals with the heart of our spiritual warfare.

I have tried to write it as simply as possible and set out many of the principles which I have learnt the past fourteen years.

I want to express my deep debt to Dr. Derek Prince through whose ministry I was encouraged to become involved in the ministry of deliverance fourteen years ago. I have used many of the principles which he expressed in his own ministry and I acknowledge this accordingly.

As I have built upon the foundation which I learnt through Dr. Derek Prince's ministry and have studied the Word of God, the Lord has liberated me in many areas of my own life. Furthermore, as the Holy Spirit has taught me and expanded my understanding of these matters I have tried to embody these understandings within the pages of this book.

It is my earnest prayer that this book will prove a great blessing to tens of thousands of Christians who are seeking a deeper walk with the Lord.

BILL SUBRITZKY

ONE

How I came into the Deliverance Ministry

BEFORE CONVERSION

For many years prior to my conversion, I attended the Anglican church of which I am still a member. During those years, many things were wrong in my life and I often let my beach home to all manner of people for all kinds of purposes.

One night, my son Paul, who was then aged 9 years, entered that beach home with us and went into his bedroom. Before switching on the light, he let out a loud scream and rushed through the house and disappeared outside. It took us one hour to find him. He was weeping, and he was a changed boy. For the next ten years he was completely changed. He was always rebellious. When he was ten years of age, the local school asked me to call and they asked me why he was so different from his sisters. At 11 years of age, he asked me if he was adopted. At 12 years of age, my wife Pat told me that if I kept him out of jail until he was twenty then I would deserve a medal.

I worked hard to do my best for Paul, but his rebellion grew. I even put him in a paramilitary organization when he was 16 years old to teach him discipline but he came back in a worse state than ever. He was aged 18 years when I finally came to the Lord one night and confessed Him publicly as my Lord and Saviour. Paul and the rest of my family were present with me. That same night he made his commitment to the Lordship of Jesus Christ with the rest of the family and we were all baptized in the Holy Spirit. Paul changed immediately. I did not understand at the time what had happened, but subsequently came to realize that when he made his commitment to Jesus Christ and was baptized in the Holy Spirit, a demon had left him. This demon had been lurking in that bedroom at my beach home when Paul had entered it nine years earlier. It had tormented him for all those years but now, at the age of eighteen, as he turned his life over to Jesus Christ and was baptized with the Holy Spirit, that demon left him. My son was now like the boy I had known during the first nine years of his life. He became a God fearing, loving son, and we have enjoyed wonderful fellowship together for the past thirteen years. He is married to a beautiful Christian wife . . . they have two lovely children, one of whom is already old enough to know Jesus as Lord.

AFTER CONVERSION

After the conversion of my wife Pat and myself and the healing of our marriage, we opened a prayer meeting in our home. This was held weekly, and after several months we began to pray for the people after the meetings. As I was praying with a person one night, I felt a certain uneasiness about that person and believed there was something around him. A pentecostal brother who was helping me said that he believed that God was giving me the gift of discernment. I began to wait upon the Holy Spirit and realized there was a spirit of fear on that person. In the name of Jesus, I commanded it to go. There was a tremendous shaking and the spirit left that person.

I then began to read all the literature I could about demons and in particular I listened to many tapes of Dr. Derek Prince, from whom I received immense help. It soon became apparent to me that many people had demonic problems. Shortly afterwards, I prayed with a man aged 40 years who had a spirit of abortion in him and he curled up like a foetus and screamed.

As others ministered with me, we saw this man totally delivered. His mother had tried to abort him while he was in the womb, hence the spirit of abortion had entered him.

By now my vicar was assisting me and many people arrived with problems. My study became like a zoo. My children who slept in adjacent rooms often told me in the morning that they had heard these animal-like sounds coming from the study. People were being delivered. The spirits of violence, hate, resentment, bitterness, lust, fear, and all manner of other demons, would leave people as we prayed together and agreed for the person's deliverance. Sometimes the people would lie down as though dead and this would cause us great fear until we understood that it was a trick of Satan to make us fearful. This reminded us of the boy whom Jesus healed, and as the spirit came out of him, he became as one dead so that many said, "He is dead".

"But Jesus took him by the hand and lifted him up, and he arose." (Mark 9:27)

On other occasions, as we prayed for people, the Holy Spirit would tell us by the gift of discernment that the spirit of insanity was present. I would pray against such a spirit by placing my hand on the forehead of the person, commanding it to go, and there would be terrible manifestations. Satan's voice would say the person was going to go mad and would remain so. However, as we took authority in the name of Jesus and commanded the demon to loose its grip from the person's mind and release all of its tentacles then the person would come absolutely free and would be a changed person in the Lord Jesus Christ.

THE COMMISSION OF JESUS

Yes, as we ministered in the power of the Holy Spirit we soon realized why on every occasion that Jesus had commissioned the disciples to preach the gospel, he also commissioned them to heal the sick and cast out devils. One commission went with the other, and we soon realized that, in order to have an effective healing ministry, we also needed an effective deliverance ministry.

I also realized I was dealing with beings who had intelligence and certain abilities, such as speech, self-awareness, knowledge, but the only way I could defeat those beings and command them to leave people would be to have the power of the Holy Spirit in my life with total dependence on the Lord Jesus Christ. I also needed a certainty in my spirit that Jesus was with me by the Holy Spirit and that His Word was absolutely true.

I came to realize that our wrestling match was not against flesh and blood but against principalities and powers and the spirits of wickedness in the heavenlies. Sometimes the deliverance will become like a wrestling match as the demons wrestle within the person and try to frighten us with their force and strength.

As I came to surrender more and more of my life to the Lordship of Jesus Christ and to read and believe the Bible as the true and inspired Word of God, I found that increased authority was given me by the Holy Spirit. I have come to realize that so much sickness is caused by demonic activity and for this reason, amongst others, I recognize the need for the ministry of deliverance in conjunction with healing.

It is my earnest desire to encourage every member of the Body of Christ to be aware of the authority that Jesus Christ has given us, and for this reason I have written this book.

TWO

The Temple of the Holy Spirit

Our body is intended to be the temple of the Holy Spirit. One of the great truths which comes to us when we yield ourselves to the Lordship of Jesus Christ and surrender to His will is the truth that our body is intended to be the temple of God's Holy Spirit. This is clearly expressed as follows:

> *"Do you not know that you are the temple of God and that the Spirit of God dwells in you?*
> *If anyone defiles the temple of God, God will destroy him. For the temple of God is holy, which temple you are."* (1 Cor.3:16,17).

And again:—

> *"Or do you not know that your body is the temple of the Holy Spirit who is in you, whom you have from God, and you are not your own?*
> *For you were bought at a price; therefore glorify God*

in your body and in your spirit, which are God's."
(1 Cor.6:19,20).

In these days of so-called liberal thinking and liberation theology, as well as the changing sexual standards, we find that there is a great break-down of moral standards. The Word of God says . . .

"Do you not know that your bodies are members of Christ? Shall I then take the members of Christ and make them members of a prostitute?
Certainly not!
Or do you not know that he who is joined to a prostitute is one body with her? For "The two," he says, "shall become one flesh."
But he who is joined to the Lord is one spirit with him.
Flee sexual immorality. Every sin that a man does is outside the body, but he who commits sexual immorality sins against his own body." (1 Cor.6:15-18).

PLAN OF SATAN

Satan's plan is to defile the temple of God's Holy Spirit. One of the most effective ways to do so is through sexual immorality. When sexual intercourse takes place outside of marriage, strong spirits or demons of lust and perverted sex can pass from one body to another during the act of sexual intercourse. People then often find that they have desires which they cannot control and need to go from one person to another seeking sexual satisfaction.

There are, of course, other ways in which the temple

of the Holy Spirit can be defiled, for example, through the smoking habit and addiction to alcohol. In these and other ways Satan attacks our body, usually by placing the desire in our mind, and if we permit it to increase then we are faced with a situation that can go out of control.

GOD'S PLAN

When we come to a knowledge of the Lord Jesus Christ, our minds should be renewed and we should receive the mind of Christ. In this way, our thought life and actions should be governed by the Holy Spirit. However, in my own experience, I find that many people, for reasons which will be discussed in this book, find great difficulty in controlling thought patterns and habits which, to say the least, are totally destructive and for this reason they need deliverance. This can apply equally to the Christian as well as to the non-Christian.

God desires to dwell in us and to walk with us.

"And what agreement has the temple of God with idols? For you are the temple of the living God. As God has said:
'I will dwell in them
And walk among them.
I will be their God,
And they shall be my people.'" (2 Cor.6:16).

God therefore requires us to walk in a holy way before Him.

"Because it is written, 'Be holy, for I am holy.'" (1 Peter 1:16).

Many Christians struggle to walk in true holiness but find great difficulty in doing so, often for reasons which they cannot understand. The purpose of this book will be to throw light on some of the reasons why these difficulties do exist.

THREE

Spiritual Warfare

Before we can go any further we need to clearly understand that there is a spiritual being named Satan who is also described in the Bible as Lucifer, or an angel of light.

> "*And no wonder! For Satan himself transforms himself into an angel of light.*" (2 Cor. 11:14)

There is also, of course, the Trinity, namely God the Father, God the Son and God the Holy Spirit, and the person who has committed themselves to Jesus Christ as Lord and Saviour has the indwelling presence of these three Persons of the Godhead.

Ever since the fall of Adam, there has been a spiritual battle going on for the possession of men's minds and spirits. The scripture is perfectly clear about the existence of Satan and his kingdom, for indeed as we read ...

"Then Jesus was led up by the Spirit into the wilderness
to be tempted by the devil." (Matt. 4:1)

And we read of His temptation. Jesus resisted and
overcame Satan by the power of the Word of God. Satan
has spiritual powers under his authority in descending
orders of authority. Thus we read in Ephesians:

"For we do not wrestle against flesh and blood, but
against principalities, against powers, against the rulers of
the darkness of this age, against spiritual hosts of wickedness
in the heavenly places." (Eph.6:12)

SATAN'S AUTHORITY OVER THE NATIONS

Satan places unseen princes and powers of the air
over every nation and city with descending orders of
authority all the way down to demons which walk on the
ground and seek a home. They have a craving to live in an
unclean body.

"When an unclean spirit goes out of a man, he goes
through dry places, seeking rest, and finds none.
"Then he says, 'I will return to my house from which I
came.' And when he comes, he finds it empty, swept, and put
in order.
"Then he goes and takes with him seven other spirits
more wicked than himself, and they enter and l   ?re;
and the last state of that man is worse than the first. So shall
it also be with this wicked generation." (Matt.12:43-45).

This is not necessarily a human body, it can be the
body of an animal:

"And all the demons begged him, saying, "Send us to the swine, that we may enter them."

And at once Jesus gave them permission. Then the unclean spirits went out and entered the swine (there were about two thousand); and the herd ran violently down the steep place into the sea, and drowned in the sea." (Mark 5:12,13).

These spirit beings seek to rule over countries, over cities, and even over churches by bringing with them hordes of demonic powers such as envy, jealousy, unbelief, pride, lust, and ambition. All of these descending orders of authority are under the control of Satan himself.

THE THREE HEAVENS

Scripture makes it clear that there is a third heaven

"I know a man in Christ who fourteen years ago — whether in the body I do not know, or whether out of the body I do not know, God knows — such a one was caught up to the third heaven." (2 Cor.12:2)

"Indeed heaven and the highest heavens belong to the LORD your GOD, also the earth with all that is in it." (Deut.10:14).

I believe there is the heaven which we see, which could be called the first heaven, but between it and the third heaven there is a second heaven, which is the seat of Satan's power and authority. We read of Jesus passing through the heavens . . .

"Seeing then that we have a great high priest who has passed through the heavens, Jesus the Son of God, let us hold fast our confession." (Heb.4:14)

DEMONIC PRINCES

Many times when I go to preach in various countries, cities or churches, I wait upon the Holy Spirit and He gives me a clear indication of the nature of the demonic power which is exercising control over that particular place. We remember the reference to such powers in Daniel Chapter 10, when Daniel was fasting for three full weeks and the angel of the Lord appeared to him with a body like beryl, his face like the appearance of lightning and his eyes like torches of fire, his arms and feet like burnished bronze in colour and the sounds of his words like the voice of a multitude. (Daniel 10:6).

This angel described how Daniel's prayers were heard by God from the very first day. The angel had come because of Daniel's prayers, but the prince of the kingdom of Persia, an angelic being, had stood against God's angel for 21 days and Michael, one of the other archangels had come to help him as he battled the demonic prince of the kingdom of Persia. The angel went on to say that he had to return to fight with the prince of Persia again and referred also to the prince of Greece, another angelic being.

These demonic princes have authority in the heavenly realms over the nations and seek to withstand the authority of the kingdom of God.

AT VANUATU

Some years ago when I visited the islands of Vanuatu in the South Pacific (formerly called the New Hebrides), I gathered together with Christians who had invited me, to pray with them. As we did so, the Lord gave me a vision of an animal rising up out of the sea, with its head facing towards the south. It had the head of a bear, ears like those of a giraffe, a mouth like a horse, hair like a goat, and nose like a horse. Above it was written the name "Division". It did not require much imagination to realize that this was the name of the ruling spirit over Vanuatu because at that time there was considerable division in those islands which were coming to independence. There were two factions seeking to gain control of the government, and the country was facing possible bloodshed.

I had come to Vanuatu at the invitation of the Anglican Bishop, Bishop Derek Rawcliffe, who invited me to speak to his entire Synod concerning the deliverance ministry. The very same day that I saw this vision, I was invited to meet with the then Prime Minister who shared with me a dream which he had some two years earlier and which he had asked many people, including the clergy, to explain but without success. He then, without further ado began to share the dream with me.

It took him about twenty minutes to tell it to me and at the conclusion he looked at me expectantly, obviously hoping that I could give him an explanation. At that moment I said to the Lord, "Lord, I am not a Daniel or a Joseph and I have never had the experience of interpreting a dream". However, the Holy Spirit seemed to speak to me at the moment and, before I knew where I was, I was in fact interpreting that dream.

The Prime Minister was intrigued with the explanation and interpretation and obviously accepted that it was correct.

ANGLICAN SYNOD

The outcome of this experience was that the next day the Prime Minister in his formal opening of the Anglican Synod commended my ministry to the whole Synod by explaining that at last his dream had been interpreted. This provided a very powerful platform from which I could minister and after two days of ministry the whole Anglican Synod (some 90 persons in all) came into the baptism of the Holy Spirit and into the gifts of the Holy Spirit. The Bishop, with me, laid hands on every member of the Synod and they all came into this experience, including the man who was subsequently to lead that country to independence without bloodshed, namely Father Walter Lini.

After I had seen the vision of that animal of division,

the Christians had prayed and fasted against it and demolished its authority by the name of Jesus, with the result that the Holy Spirit could move freely in those circumstances. I firmly believe that the obedience of the Christians on that occasion in praying and fasting and using the authority in the name of Jesus to bring down that spirit of division, contributed mightily to the subsequent peaceful outcome of the transition into independence of that nation.

REVIVAL

Another result was that the Anglican clergy went back to their parishes throughout Vanuatu and encouraged their congregations to commit their lives fully to Jesus Christ and those who needed to were born again in the Spirit of God. The clergy then encouraged their congregations to move in the gifts of the Holy Spirit referred to in 1 Corinthians 12, namely the word of wisdom, the word of knowledge, the gift of faith, the gifts of healing, working of miracles, discerning of spirits, gift of prophecy, gifts of tongues and interpretation of tongues. The result was that the evensong, instead of lasting one hour on a Sunday evening, went on to the early hours of the next morning as people were healed and delivered from demon power as their lives were transformed by the power of the gospel of Jesus Christ. The effect of this revival spread into the Solomon Islands, where it is still being felt.

GOD'S HEALING POWER

In another incident in the same crusades which I conducted at Vanuatu, a leading member of one of the denominations who had been opposed to the baptism of the Holy Spirit, attended one of the meetings. There were approximately 1,000 people present and, after I had preached, the Holy Spirit, by the word of knowledge, indicated that there was a man at the back of the meeting who needed to be healed from a bowel condition. I went there and pointed to the man saying that the Holy Spirit desired that he should be healed. I walked back to the front of the meeting but the man had not moved. The Holy Spirit then indicated that I should again go to the back of the meeting and ask the man to come forward. I did a second time and as I walked to the front of the meeting I noticed he had still not come out. As I went to speak again, the Holy Spirit told me that I must go back again, and for the third time I walked right through the meeting to the back and pointed to the man. He did not appear to move but on the way back as I looked over my shoulder, I noticed he was slowly following me.

When he had reached the front of the meeting, I prayed for him and he was taken to the ground by the power of the Holy Spirit. He lay on the ground for over an hour while I continued to pray for other people. After he had stood on his feet, I asked him to describe what had happened. He could not speak for he was weeping so profusely. I left him alone for a further 30 minutes and then returned to him. He was then able to explain to the gathering that, when I laid hands on him and he went down on to the floor, a great white light came around him and a voice spoke to him telling him he was healed. He had in fact had a bowel condition for over thirteen years and was coming to New Zealand that very month to have an operation. Like every person who knows they have had an instantaneous healing, he knew that in fact he had been healed.

The following Sunday morning he stood up in his church and proclaimed that the charismatic renewal to which he had been so opposed was indeed a move of the Holy Spirit, and from henceforth he would be supporting this move. He too was baptized in the Holy Spirit. As a result of this episode the whole denomination opened to the power of the Holy Spirit.

It is thus clear that when we stand against these spiritual powers, then we are able to defeat them.

Do it in the authority of the name of Jesus. He Himself commissioned us . . .

> "Then Jesus came and spoke to them, saying, 'All authority has been given to me in heaven and in earth.
> Go therefore and make disciples of all the nations, baptizing them in the name of the Father and of the Son and of the Holy Spirit.'" (Matthew 28:18,19).

It is clear from this scripture that the authority which has been given to Jesus has in turn been given to his disciples. We are His disciples.

AT SINGAPORE

When ministering in Singapore some years ago Bishop Chiu, who was the Anglican Bishop, invited me to conduct a seminar on the deliverance ministry. Half way through the seminar he interrupted me to say he believed that there were demons in the cathedral. I had felt that this was so during the course of the meetings but decided to say nothing until the Holy Spirit showed this to Bishop Chiu. As the bishop spoke these words indicating that he believed there were demons in the cathedral, the Holy Spirit showed me a black angel of death some three metres high, over the top of the cathedral. I saw it clearly in my spirit and I indicated as much to Bishop Chiu. He immediately exclaimed, "Bill, I have no difficulty in accepting this. During the war years the Japanese took all the Australian nurses in Singapore, brought them to the grounds of this cathedral and massacred them. They were buried in the grounds of this cathedral during the war and exhumed after the war had ended."

It was clear that, following that terrible event, Satan had placed this angel of death over the cathedral and was seeking to bind the power of the Holy Spirit being exercised in the cathedral. We decided to form a procession and march around the cathedral Jericho-style. As we came opposite the place where the nurses had been buried, I heard the sound as of a rushing wind and the power of the Holy Spirit came down the side of the cathedral touching Bishop Chiu who began to go down under the power of the Holy Spirit. It was clear from the tremendous anointing which fell at that time that the angel of death had been removed from the top of that cathedral.

Subsequently we entered the cathedral and commanded every demon power which had been in that place under the authority of the angel of death to depart.

I believe that one of the reasons why renewal has been so mightily manifested in the diocese of Singapore under Bishop Chiu, and now under Bishop Moses Tay, has been because the Christians have taken authority over the demon powers which would have bound that cathedral. This surely is a lesson to us all, to pray and fast and to be spiritually alert to any forces of Satan which would seek to take authority over our country, city or church. Sometimes when I enter a city to preach, I see clearly in my spirit demonic forces such as lust, pride and envy exercising control over that city.

Similarly, in many churches there can be spirits of division, jealousy and other forces operating because Satan has sought to place some demonic angel over that church in order to render it powerless.

SPIRIT OF SECTARIANISM

Another very common prince which Satan seeks to place over denominations and churches is the spirit of sectarianism. This spirit deceives the members of that denomination or church by a deceiving demon which tells that church that it has the whole truth and that other denominations or churches are wrong. Sometimes it infers that that church has a greater measure of the truth than other churches. This may well be true in the sense that the church may be more biblically based than other churches or denominations. However, in this way, Satan speaks through the spirit of pride; it produces the spirit of rebellion which causes that particular church or denomination to refrain from fellowship with other members of the body of Christ. This, of course, grieves the Holy Spirit because it is contrary to the Word of God and particularly the unity of the brethren. We remember the great High Priestly prayer of Jesus Christ in John 17 . . .

> *"That they all may be one, as you, Father, are in me, and I in you; that they also may be one in us, that the world may believe that you sent me."* (John 17:21).

We remember, too, the words in Psalm 133:1 and 3B.

> *"Behold, how good and how pleasant it is*
> *For brethren to dwell together in unity!*
> *For there the Lord commanded the blessing — Life forevermore."*

One of the great ruses of Satan is to keep division within the body of Christ so that its unity cannot be perceived by the world.

We must at all times be aware that we are in spiritual warfare and that Satan does not leave us alone simply because we have committed our lives to Jesus Christ. If anything, he seeks to attack us with even more vehemence, particularly those places in which we worship as he seeks to reinstate his own authority again.

MINISTERING ANGELS

Let us realize, however, that we have the victory and that we do have ministering angels which are sent to minister to us . . .

> "Are they not all ministering spirits sent forth to minister for those who will inherit salvation?" (Heb. 1:14).

If we remain faithful to the word and the Spirit of the living Christ, then we will be aware of the spiritual armour necessary to defeat Satan. We find this spiritual armour set out in Ephesians 6:13-18, namely the girdle of truth, the breastplate of righteousness and having our feet shod with the preparation of the gospel of peace. Above all, we should take the shield of faith, so that we can stand against the fiery darts of the wicked one and the helmet of salvation should be placed over our mind. We need to be familiar with the sword of the Spirit which is the Word of God, so that we can use it as an offensive weapon against the enemy in the same way that Jesus did when Satan tempted Him.

We should always pray with all prayer and supplication in the Holy Spirit. 1 Corinthians 14:14 makes it clear that if we pray in a tongue, our spirit prays. For this reason, it is wonderful to be baptized in the Holy Spirit and to release our tongue to God so that we can use our Holy Spirit tongue in defying the enemy. The Holy Spirit has free play in praying through us to God and in this way defeating the power of the enemy. But praise God, Jesus Christ has won the battle!

> "Having disarmed principalities and powers, he made a public spectacle of them, triumphing over them in it." (Col. 2:15).

Yes, Jesus has triumphed over the principalities and powers of the air and we have authority to stand in His name and command them to bow down to the name of Jesus.

However, although Jesus has won the victory, we are required to appropriate that victory in the same way as we appropriate salvation, namely, we must act upon what Jesus has done for us and then we will find that the enemy will flee.

FOUR

The Strong Men

It is necessary for us to understand that, in this battle against principalities and powers, we are battling against strong men of varying degrees of authority. Jesus made it clear that it is necessary to bind the strong man before we can enter his house and plunder his goods. Many people are bound by a strong man in their life, whether it be lust, fornication, unclean thoughts, addictions, fear, resentment, unforgiveness, or any other form of strong man. Jesus said:

"Or else how can one enter a strong man's house and plunder his goods, unless he first binds the strong man? And then he will plunder his house." (Matt. 12:29).

It is therefore necessary to bind the strong man but we need to know against whom we are fighting. Paul said he did not beat the air, he did not run with uncertainty.

"Therefore I run thus: not with uncertainty. Thus I fight: not as one who beats the air." (1 Cor.9:26).

Paul knew exactly who was his enemy. We all know it is Satan, but we also need to understand the strong men who are under Satan's authority.

There are three particular strong men referred to in scripture. We of course understand that, in the spirit, there is neither man nor woman, male nor female, and the term "strong men" can refer to either male or female in the spirit.

These strong men are:

SPIRIT OF JEZEBEL

This spirit which is a powerful prince of the air is revealed in particular in Isaiah 47. The prophet Isaiah refers to her through the Holy Spirit as "the virgin daughter of Babylon" and he is speaking to a great spiritual power of the air over Babylon. She has been called "The lady of kingdoms".

Read what Isaiah says:

"Therefore hear this now, you who are given to pleasures,
Who dwell securely,
Who say in your heart,
'I am, and there is no one else besides me;
I shall not sit as a widow,
Nor shall I know the loss of children';" (Isaiah 47:8)

Truly, she considers herself in place of God by

saying, "I am, and none else beside me", and also she has children. However, she will know the loss of those children:

> "But these two things shall come to you
> In a moment, in one day:
> The loss of children, and widowhood.
> They shall come upon you in their fullness
> Because of the multitude of your sorceries,
> For the great abundance of your enchantments."
> (Isaiah 47:9)

We find in Revelation 17 and 18, confirmation of the scripture. We see the woman arrayed in purple and adorned with precious stones and pearls, having in her hand a golden cup full of fornications and filthiness of her fornication:

> "The woman was arrayed in purple and scarlet, and adorned with gold and precious stones and pearls, having in her hand a golden cup full of abominations and the filthiness of her fornication." (Revelation 17:4).

BABYLON THE GREAT

She was named Babylon the Great, the mother of harlots and abominations of the world:

> "and on her forehead a name was written:
> 'MYSTERY,
> BABYLON THE GREAT,
> THE MOTHER OF PROSTITUTES
> AND OF THE ABOMINATIONS
> OF THE EARTH.'"
> (Revelation 17:5)

We find the words of Isaiah repeated in Revelation 18:

> *"In the measure that she glorified herself and lived luxuriously, in the same measure give her torment and sorrow; for she says in her heart, 'I sit as queen, and am no widow, and will not see sorrow.'*
> *"Therefore her plagues will come in one day — death and mourning and famine. And she will be utterly burned with fire, for strong is the Lord God who judges her."* (Revelation 18:7,8).

It is noteworthy that she is the first of the strong men to be cast into the lake of fire and brimstone.

This great harlot spirit which today is manifesting more and more in the world has been one which is difficult to see and to understand. In fact, in Isaiah 47 she says, "None seeth me".

> *"For you have trusted in your wickedness;*
> *You have said, 'No one sees me';*
> *Your wisdom and your knowledge have warped you;*
> *And you have said in your heart,*
> *'I am, and there is no one else besides me.'"* (Isaiah 47:10)

Obviously she is a spirit of great pride and believes that she has been able to hide from everybody.

FEMINISM

It is this great harlot spirit which is manifesting in the world today through extremes of feminism. As we have already seen from the scripture referred to, she is involved in sorcery and enchantments, also she is involved in astrology, stargazing and horoscopes:

> *"You are wearied in the multitude of your counsels;*
> *Let now the astrologers, the stargazers,*
> *And the monthly prognosticators*
> *Stand up and save you*
> *From these things that shall come upon you."*
> *(Isaiah 47.13).*

This great spirit which, up to this generation, has manifested so widely is now exposing herself more and more through the drug culture, rock music, marital breakdown, pornography, and every conceivable form of lust and filthiness; hence she is called the Mother of Abominations.

This is the great demonic spirit that is increasingly coming upon the world in these last days. She is one of the princes of the air against which we need to stand.

She is in direct opposition to the will of God, being based totally upon idolatry and disobedience to the first and second commandment of God.

CHURCH AT THYATIRA

In Revelation Chapter 2 we find her again referred to when Jesus Christ is talking about the church at Thyatira. While he is referring specifically to a woman in the flesh he is also referring to the spirit that is operating through that woman and effecting that church. Consequently he pronounced judgement upon her if she persisted with her conduct because she was affecting the whole church.

> "Nevertheless I have a few things against you, because you allow that woman Jezebel, who calls herself a prophetess, to teach and beguile my servants to commit sexual immorality and to eat things sacrificed to idols.
>
> "And I gave her time to repent of her sexual immorality, and she did not repent.
>
> "Indeed I will cast her into a sickbed, and those who commit adultery with her into great tribulation, unless they repent of their deeds.
>
> "And I will kill her children with death. And all the churches shall know that I am he who searches the minds and hearts. And I will give to each one of you according to your works.
>
> "But to you I say, and to the rest in Thyatira, as many as do not have this doctrine, and who have not known the depths of Satan, as they call them, I will put on you no other burden." (Revelation 2:20-24)

HER CHILDREN

From my own experience in following a search of the scriptures, I have concluded that some of her children are as follows. I do not suggest that the list is necessarily correct in every respect or exhaustive, and may be the Holy Spirit will guide the reader further in this area, but I have found from experience that if we bind this great power of the air by agreement with others, then we can expect to see real deliverance as far as churches and individuals are concerned. I suggest her children are:

Addictions, apostasy and divisions in the church, adultery, arrogance, broken marriages, charms, DECEPTION, divination, domination, drugs, fear, feminism, filthiness (of the spirit and of the flesh), fornication, free love, hatred, harlotry, heresies, homosexuality, idolatry, incest and indecency (this comes as a result of a curse from a previous generation involved in idolatry), jealousy, lasciviousness, lust, unclean thoughts, masturbation, occultic things, perverted sexual acts, oral sex, false religion and heresies (e.g., Mormonism, Jehovah's Witnesses, Herbert Armstrong, Children of God), pride, sorcery, spiritism, spiritual blindness (e.g., Freemasonry, Mormonism); spirit of religion, witchcraft, i.e., domination, lying, blasphemy, covetousness, secular humanism, permissiveness and all occultic involvements.

The ruling spirit under Jezebel is DECEPTION.

SPIRIT OF ANTI-CHRIST

The second great strong man manifesting increasingly in the world today is the spirit of Anti-Christ. John referred to the spirit in his first letter, Chapter 4:

"And this is the spirit of the Antichrist, which you have heard was coming, and is now already in the world." (1 John 4:3)

We are aware that this spirit in the last days will manifest as the man of sin, or the beast. We find this clearly referred to in 2 Thessalonians:

"Let no one deceive you by any means; for that day will not come unless the falling away comes first, and the

man of sin is revealed, the son of perdition,
  *who opposes and exalts himself above all that is called
God or that is worshipped, so that he sits as God in the
temple of God, showing himself that he is God." (2 Thess.
2:3,4)*

One of the attributes of this man of sin, or the
Anti-Christ, will be that he sits as God in the temple of
God in Jerusalem during the last days.

LAWLESS ONE

He is also referred to as "the lawless one" and is
restrained by the Holy Spirit:

*"For the mystery of lawlessness is already at work;
only he who now restrains will do so until he is taken out of
the way.*
  *And then the lawless one will be revealed, whom the
Lord will consume with the breath of his mouth and
destroy with the brightness of his coming.*
  *The coming of the lawless one is according to the
working of Satan, with all power, signs, and lying wonders." (2 Thess. 2:7-9).*

The manifestation of the spirit today is increasing in
the world, particularly in rock festivals and with rock
bands.

Recently in our city, we had a visit from a band called
"The Police Band". This band had taken the name of
authority, namely the police. Many people were con-
fused when they sought to make arrangements to

attend the performance. They tried to order seats through the local police station! This band had taken the name of authority, and when it went into the main arena to perform, the players sat on the stage in the position of authority, namely by taking the name of authority, the police. This particular band boasts that it specializes in creating scenes of violence, and injury often results. On this particular occasion, the police in our city stated publicly that they could not control the lawlessness which followed that band. The spirit of lawlessness was with the band and manifested violently. A girl was gang-raped on her way into the stadium, buses were overturned, cars were burned, and the crowd went wild. This is a clear manifestation of the power of the spirit of Anti-Christ followed by lawlessness, which we will see increasingly during these latter days. Thank God, we have the power of the Holy Spirit within us and that He is restraining the power of lawlessness during these latter days as we pray.

INTERVENTION BY GOD

When I was preaching at a rock festival recently, the spirit of lawlessness began to manifest more and more through the presence of a rock band on the stage. I was present with a large Christian contingent, who were seeking to evangelize a crowd of some 40,000. It was unsafe to walk through the main arena while the rock bands were playing, especially the one which promoted the most violence. Beer cans were thrown, people were urinated upon . . . there was a tremendous spirit of violence. That night, one of the policemen came to the Christian tent. He was Christian himself. He said that unless the violence could be stopped that night, there was no way in which the police could control the crowd, and if they went wild, people would be killed!

The Christians got down on their knees and began to pray, binding the spirit of lawlessness. One of them had a vision of horsemen coming down over the whole arena, precisely at 7.30 pm that night, and we knew that the power of God was being manifested in withholding the spirit of lawlessness.

The crowd quietened, although we at the Christian tent did not know exactly what was happening except in our spirit. It was interesting to note that in the newspaper the following day, there was a report that at 7.30 p.m., just when the crowd seemed to become out of hand, and were about to go beserk, suddenly the whole crowd fell into silence. The spirit of lawlessness had been overcome!

The rest of the concert was conducted in a comparatively orderly manner.

How wonderful it is when we ally ourselves with the power of the Holy Spirit to bind these strong men.

CHILDREN OF ANTI-CHRIST

I suggest that a list of children of this particular

strong man, namely Anti-Christ can be as follows:

> *Spirits of anger, bitterness, blasphemy, corrupt communications, curses, dissension, drunkenness, envy or hatred, fear, filthy language, lack of faith, lying, malice, murder, nightmares, outbursts of wrath, poverty, rebellion, spirit of wretchedness, rejection, selfish ambitions, stealing, strife, torment, unbelief, unforgiveness, anti-semitism, marxism and Islam.*

We find that the beast in the form of the Anti-Christ at the end of time is captured with the false prophet and is cast alive into the lake of fire burning with brimstone:

> *"Then the beast was captured, and with him the false prophet who worked signs in his presence, by which he deceived those who received the mark of the beast and those who worshipped his image. These two were cast alive into the lake of fire burning with brimstone."* (Revelation 19:20)

This is the second of the great strong men to go into the lake of fire and brimstone.

DEATH AND HELL

In the course of ministry in the deliverance area, I have often found in the past that, when I commanded the spirit's name, Death and Hell, to leave a person, violent manifestations occurred. As I began to research this area, I realized that Death and Hell were themselves strong men and are clearly referred to as such in scripture. Not only is Hades a place, but Death and Hades are demonic angels.

We find in the Book of Revelation that they, too, are cast into the lake of fire and brimstone, being the third order of strong men to go in:

> *"The sea gave up the dead who were in it, and Death and Hades delivered up the dead who were in them. And they were judged, each one according to his works.*
> *Then Death and Hades were cast into the lake of fire. This is the second death."* (Revelation 20:13,14).

CHURCHES ATTACKED

I believe that churches and individuals are attacked in turn by the spirit of Jezebel, then Anti-Christ, and finally Death and Hell brings in sickness. One of the children of Death and Hell is the spirit of curse. We know that these are curses of God, referred to in Deuteronomy 27 and 28 for the disobedient, and although there are curses of the law and have been dealt with by Jesus on the cross (Galations 3:13) we need to appropriate what Jesus Christ has done on the cross when we turn to Him.

> *"Christ has redeemed us from the curse of the law, having become a curse for us (for it is written, 'Cursed is everyone who hangs on a tree')"*

As we turn to Christ, then the spirits of these curses can be removed.

Sometimes curses are placed by people who are operating in the demonic realm. Gypsies and others have always exercised powers of cursing. Similarly, many native cultures do the same thing.

CURSES

I have come to understand that such things as frequent accidents, suicides, and successions of deaths in families and many forms of sickness could be the result of a curse.

If we know that the curse is from another person, we need to remember and act upon the words of Jesus:

"... *bless those who curse you, do good to those who hate you, and pray for those who spitefully use you and persecute you.*" (Matt. 5:44)

CHILDREN OF DEATH AND HELL

I believe that the children of Death and Hell are as follows:

Sickness, pain, plagues, breathing problems, spirits of infirmity, spirits of guilt, spirits of condemnation and fear, curses, spirits of suicide and self destruction.

Under "sickness", I would include all forms of sickness, particularly those of longstanding origin.

UNHOLY TRINITY

It has been suggested that the foregoing three strong men, namely the spirit of Jezebel, Anti-Christ, and Death andHell, are the satanic counterparts of the Holy

Trinity; namely that the spirit of Jezebel seeks to take the place of the Holy Spirit, and the spirit of Anti-Christ seeks to take the place of God the Father, and the spirit of Death and Hell seeks to take the place of Christ. It is noteworthy that they are cast into the lake of fire and brimstone in the order of Jezebel, Anti-Christ, and Death and Hell, and it does seem important in the area of ministry to cast them out in that order when they are affecting an individual or church.

These are very strong men and we must always remember the power of agreement referred to in Matthew 18:

> "Assuredly, I say to you, whatever you bind on earth will be bound in heaven, and whatever you loose on earth will be loosed in heaven." (Matt. 18:18).

As we, as Christians, agree together to bind these spiritual forces then they in turn lose their grip over the church or persons, or city, and then we can plunder their house and cast out their children.

FIVE

Can a Christian have a demon?

The answer is emphatically yes! If you have been taught that this is not so, then please keep reading and let the Holy Spirit guide you in this matter.

I am aware that there has been much teaching to the effect that Christians cannot have demons, but from my own experience in ministering during the past fourteen years I have found that to be totally incorrect.

CORRECT TRANSLATION

In the first place, we should understand clearly that you can have a demon without being demon possessed. The King James Version incorrectly translates the word "demonized" as "possessed" and this leaves people with the impression that if they have a spirit attacking them, or if they have a demon, then they are possessed by a demon. There is nothing in the Greek translation to support the word "possessed". Scholars make the point that the use of this word has frightened many people who think that if they have a demon, then they are "possessed". There can of course be true demon possession when a person's whole personality and being are given over to the influence and total possession by demonic forces, but in my experience this is comparatively rare. The more correct translation is shown in scriptures such as:

"Now there was a man in their synagogue with an unclean spirit; . . ." (Mark 1:23)

Another correct form is to describe a person as "having a demon":

"For John came neither eating nor drinking, and they say, 'He has a demon'." (Matt. 11:18)

"For a woman whose young daughter had an unclean spirit heard about him, and she came and fell at his feet." (Mark 7:25).

Some people recoil at the thought that our body can simultaneously be inhabited both by the Holy Spirit and by a demon. Only God knows the true state of a person's heart, and although many profess to have totally yielded their lives in every respect to Jesus Christ, nevertheless at times we find that certain sinful attitudes persist within believers and this gives ground for Satan to have a foothold.

SPIRIT-FILLED BELIEVERS

I have ministered to thousands of Spirit-filled believers of many years standing who have been attacked by, and were under the influence of forces which they could not understand. For example, a Pentecostal pastor of some twenty years' experience, in good standing in his church, came to me on one occasion because of a breathing problem. As I prayed with him, the Holy Spirit indicated that the source of the problem was a demon. As I came against this demon of affliction in the name of Jesus, the spirit spoke out of this man and said that it would not leave him as this had been his house for over thirty years. In response to further ministry, the demon finally left with a great scream, but not before it was identified as the demon of monkey god. This particular pastor came from a Hindu background and this monkey god which his ancestors had worshipped over many years had followed him and entered his body at conception, with the result that it had brought with it a spirit of sickness. After further prayer, the pastor was completely delivered from the spirit and was set free from the asthmatic problem which had bothered him for so long. This man had been born again and preached the gospel for many years, having been baptized in the Holy Spirit at a young age and was leading a good life. However this demonic power had found a place in his body from before birth.

On another occasion I was invited to speak at a conference of a Spirit-filled organization involving members from many denominations from all around that country. On the first evening I made a call for repentance and among the people who came out was the secretary's son, aged 33 years. The father came to me afterwards and rejoiced that his son had responded to the repentance call. He said that his son seemed to have problems which would not yield to ministry. His son had been brought up in a Pentecostal church from birth but there seemed to be some intractable problems binding him.

EXPERIENCES AT CONVENTIONS

There were two of us ministering at this convention, and as the other speaker finished the following night we stood together at the front of the platform prepared to minister to those in the convention. Without warning, a dreadful sound started up from one side of the meeting and I looked over to see the 33 year old son of the secretary manifesting in a terrible manner. His arms and legs were flying about and he was screaming in an incoherent fashion. Suddenly he seemed to leap in the air and travel in a supernatural way some ten metres towards us at about two metres off the ground. The other preacher yelled out to me, "Get out of the way, Bill!" We jumped out of the way and this man fell on the ground in the very place where we had been standing.

Some eight men jumped on him to try to hold him down as these dreadful noises came from him.

The other speaker told me that I should minister in this situation, so taking authority in the name of Jesus, I asked the men to get off this young man and I commanded the demon to be quiet. The man lay there and, as I prayed for him his eyes became tightly closed because the demons did not want to see me looking at him. By forcing the eyelids up, I could clearly see the demons in the man's eyes. He then began to wriggle backwards like a snake in front of 400 people who were assembled. He disappeared under various chairs and tables but, during the following hour, he was completely delivered. The only person objecting to the deliverance was a woman spiritist who had heard me speak on a radio programme earlier in the day. Without invitation she walked into the meeting during the course of the deliverance, obviously drawn by the spirit which was within her. She objected violently to the ministry but I soon found that she was a spiritist, and told her to keep quiet.

Finally the man was delivered and stood up praising God, knowing that all the demon power had left him. The next morning, he stood before the convention and gave his testimony. He knew he was now free from all the forces which had been operating within him and twisting his life and tormenting him. I subsequently prayed for nearly every local leader in that organization as they all sought deliverance from spirits binding them.

Following that particular convention, I was invited along with the other speaker to attend a similar convention held in another part of the same country. This convention also consisted of Spirit-filled Christians, all of whom claimed to be baptized in the Holy Spirit. There were some 500 people present. As we arrived, we were told that the topic for this particular convention was to be "Freedom from Oppressive Spirits". We felt that we had seen enough of demons for a while but now we were being called to minister again in this dimension.

Following a two hour teaching session, when we described the effect of demonic powers on people and how demons operate, a number of people came to me and asked whether I felt that they were bound by oppressive spirits. I suggested to the other speaker that, at the conclusion of his talk, we should perhaps have a mass prayer for deliverance. In due course, he completed his talk and then invited those who felt that they had problems to come forward. Approximately 100 of those present came and stood at the front of the meeting. The other speaker had to leave immediately due to a further engagement, and I was left with these people waiting for help. I called on the Lord Jesus Christ to guide me and was given clear direction to take authority over the demon powers, binding them. As I did so in the name of Jesus, many of the people fell to the ground with demons manifesting in a dramatic way. Some slithered as snakes, others were screaming, and altogether it was an incredible sight.

I stood in front of groups of ten at a time and commanded the demons to be bound in the name of Jesus. With some people, the Lord clearly indicated the source of the problem, namely wrong relationships and wrong attitudes to parents, and the demons left screaming as we took authority in these areas.

Due to the shortage of time, we were able to minister to the people for only about one hour, but fortunately there was a brother there who had experience in this ministry and, to the best of my knowledge, he was still ministering to some of these people several months later.

All of these people came from Spirit-filled churches which claimed the baptism in the Holy Spirit but you can be sure that their local churches no longer teach that Christians cannot have demons.

SICKNESS

If we accept that the source of much sickness is from the devil, then we must also accept that Christians who have sickness in their body could have spirits attacking them which are from the devil.

We remember the woman who was bound by the spirit of infirmity for eighteen years and was bent over and could in no way raise herself up:

> "But when Jesus saw her, he called her to him and said to her, 'Woman, you are loosed from your infirmity.'
>
> And he laid his hands on her, and immediately she was made straight, and glorified God." (Luke 13:12,13).

My experience of such sicknesses as asthma, arthritis, cancer and heart attacks is that they can have a demonic source. When the sufferer is properly counselled in the area of repentance, particularly in the area of forgiveness and relationships with other people, then the Holy Spirit is free to act in the power of healing. In the case of a child suffering from asthma, oftentimes the spirit enters the child through disagreement on the part of the parents. When they are properly counselled, the spirit departs from the child. Sometimes of course the spirit is of an hereditary nature and has come down through several generations. We sometimes find, for example, that the spirit of asthma has been present in earlier generations, having entered through sin on the part of some earlier member of the family. When this power is cut off in the name of Jesus, then the spirit of asthma leaves the sufferer.

SPIRITUAL WARFARE

To sum up, we are in spiritual warfare. Even though we have turned our hearts and minds over to God and seek to yield to Him, there can be hereditary spirits which bind us and from which we need deliverance. It is noteworthy that the gift of discernment of spirits in 1 Corinthians 12, like the other gifts referred to in that chapter, is for the body of Christ. In other words, the gift is there to discern spiritual forces which are attacking members of Christ's body, namely our fellow Christians, and when they come for help we must be able to discern these spirits. Too often, I find that people who should be receiving help in their own churches are bound by demonic forces which are affecting their personality or their physical wellbeing, or both. Because their churches do not operate in the deliverance ministry, these people remain bound until they seek help elsewhere. They are prayed for without result because those praying for them do not believe that a Christian can have a demon. When the spiritual forces attacking them are properly discerned, then they are set free and are able to say, "Hallelujah . . . Jesus is indeed Lord!" Jesus went about healing all who were oppressed of the devil (Acts 10:38). The devil has not ceased to try to oppress the Christians, so let us be aware that this ministry is just as valid as in the days of the early church.

MASONIC LODGE

Another form of hereditary oppression can come through the Masonic Lodge. This Lodge which worships the gods of Baal and Ashtaroth, was founded in England

In 1717 as a universal religion. Jesus is not central and the oaths taken are totally contrary to the Word of God. The person whose parents have belonged to that Lodge may well find that they are under a spirit of oppression. Until they renounce the involvement of their parents or ancestors in that Lodge, forgive their parents and ancestors and command the familiar spirit of Freemasonry to depart, they will find there is an occultic influence over them. They will have difficulty in witnessing to the presence and power of God in their lives. Many well meaning Christians belong to the Free-masonry Lodge without realizing its origin and the source of oppression upon them.

I well recall a leading member of a Christian organi-zation who came to me because he and his wife were having some problems. The Holy Spirit quickly showed that this man had been a member of the Freemasonry Lodge approximately twentyfive years earlier, and although he had left the Lodge he had never formally severed his connections with it, and in fact still had some of the regalia in his home. Like the other persons referred to earlier, this man was a Spirit-filled, tongue-speaking Christian of high standing in a Pentecostal church. He readily agreed to renounce again all involve-ment with the Freemasonry Lodge and to burn the regalia. After he had made this renunciation and the deliverance ministry commenced, a demon clearly manifested itself through this man. It threw him on the floor like a snake and he slithered along the floor and up the wall of the bedroom. His wife was horrified. Finally the demon left him. The power of the strong man had been bound and, as often happens in the deliverance ministry, the man was left weak after the strong man had departed. We prayed again that he be filled with the Holy Spirit. He rested for approximately two hours before he regained his full strength.

I met him one year later and both he and his wife were changed persons. They were rejoicing in the fullness of the power of the Holy Spirit. The demonic force of Freemasonry had so bound this man that even though he had left the Lodge, their marriage had been seriously disturbed. Now there was tremendous healing and rejoicing because the power of the Holy Spirit was able to fully operate in their lives.

Yes, we can be free. Rejoice, saith the Lord, for we can be free!

Our body is intended to be the temple of the Holy Spirit. Only God knows the state of our heart,

> ". . . *For the Lord does not see as man sees; for man looks at the outward appearance, but the Lord looks at the heart.*" (1 Sam.16:7).

OUR HEART

Our heart itself can be described like a house.

> "*The spirit of a man is the lamp of the Lord,*

Searching all the inner depths of his heart." (rooms of the belly) (Proverbs 20:27)

We can open one door and let Jesus come in as Saviour, but have we let Him in fully as Lord? This involves opening all the dark recesses of our heart to the power of the Holy Spirit. Some of us stop short of doing this and hold within our heart envy, jealousy, fear, rebellion, unforgiveness, and other wrong attitudes which in turn give Satan power to operate in our lives and bring in his demon powers. In Acts 5:3, we read the words of Peter, "Ananias, why has Satan filled your heart to lie to the Holy Spirit, and keep back part of the price of the land for yourself?"

Peter discerned a wrong spirit on the part of both Ananias and Sapphira with the result that they both died. It is noteworthy that they were followers of JESUS CHRIST or what we later called Christians.

Yes, as we have said in the foregoing, we are in spiritual warfare. Satan is a legalist, and if he can find any legal ground on which he can establish his right to occupy part of our being because of sin, then he will immediately occupy that ground. Even God Himself will permit a Christian to be attacked when the Christian is unforgiving.

"And his master was angry, and delivered him to the torturers until he should pay all that was due to him.
"So my heavenly Father also will do to you if each of

you, from his heart, does not forgive his brother his trespasses." (Matt. 18:34,35)

The torturers referred to here are clearly demons. It is therefore clear that we must walk before God in true repentance and continue to resist the devil. It is also clear that Christians can have demons sometimes from inheritance as the result of the sins of their parents or forefathers and sometimes as a result of their own sins. Thus we have the need for the gift of discernment of spirits in the body of Christ to help discern these demon powers and see the other members of the body of Christ set free.

SIX

The Area of the Flesh

It is important to distinguish between the works of the flesh and the works of the devil.

The Bible describes our old nature in various ways. This is the old nature of Adam with which we are all born and which needs to be crucified upon the cross of Jesus Christ. The old nature of man is in rebellion against God and it is only when we are converted and born again of the Spirit of God that we can begin to know the defeat of the old man.

BAPTISM

As Paul says in Romans Chapter 6:

"Therefore we were buried with him through baptism into death, that just as Christ was raised from the dead by the glory of the Father, even so we also should walk in newness of life.

For if we have been united together in the likeness of

his death, certainly we also shall be in the likeness of his resurrection,

knowing this, that our old man was crucified with him, that the body of sin might be done away with, that we should no longer be slaves of sin." (Romans 6:4-6).

Many people will blame demons for their own lack of self control and for their failure to put the old nature under the cross of Jesus Christ. The only way the old man can be dealt with is through the cross of Jesus Christ, and we need to crucify the old man daily.

Continuing in the same chapter of Romans, Paul says:

"Likewise you also, reckon yourselves to be dead indeed to sin, but alive to God in Christ Jesus our Lord.

Therefore do not let sin reign in your mortal body, that you should obey it in its lusts.

And do not present your members as instruments of unrighteousness to sin, but present yourselves to God as being alive from the dead, and your members as instruments of righteousness to God.

For sin shall not have dominion over you, for you are not under law but under grace." (Romans 6:11-14)

The foregoing scriptures show a clear exercise of our will. This will must be exercised if we are to walk as the scripture commands us to walk. We are not to let sin take over our body, either through our life or in any other way, but we are to walk in the power of the Holy Spirit daily and defeat the power of sin in our lives.

The scripture requires us to become slaves of God, have fruit to holiness, that we may have everlasting life:

> "But now having been set free from sin, and having become slaves of God, you have your fruit to holiness, and the end, everlasting life." (Romans 6:22).

FRUIT OF SPIRIT

We must daily seek for the fruit of the Holy Spirit to operate in our lives as we yield to Jesus Christ. However, there is a battle taking place between our flesh and the Holy Spirit.

> "I say then: Walk in the Spirit, and you shall not fulfill the lust of the flesh.
> For the flesh lusts against the Spirit, and the Spirit against the flesh; and these are contrary to one another, so that you do not do the things that you wish.
> But if you are led by the Spirit, you are not under the law.
> Now the works of the flesh are evident, which are: adultery, fornication, uncleanness, licentiousness, idolatry, sorcery, hatred, contentions, jealousies, outbursts of wrath, selfish ambitions, dissensions, heresies, envy, murders, drunkenness, revels, and the like; of which I tell you beforehand, just as I also told you in time past, that those who practise such things will not inherit the kingdom of God." (Galatians 5:16-21).

If we walk in the Spirit, then we have the fruit of the Holy Spirit, which is love, joy, peace, longsuffering, kindness, goodness, faithfulness, gentleness, self control.

When the fruit of the Spirit is operating and is flowering in our life, there is little opportunity for demon activity to manifest.

As we have said previously, we are engaged in spiritual warfare and we remember the scriptures from 1 Peter:

"If the righteous one is scarcely saved,
Where will the ungodly and the sinner appear?"
(1 *Peter* 4:18).

NARROW WAY

Yes, the way is a narrow way, and although many are called, few are chosen because they do not allow Jesus to be Lord of their lives. Many succumb to the old ways and go back into the world. While we are in the world we are not of the world, and although we must maintain an attitude of love at all times towards all people, let us not fall into the trap of becoming part of the world, thus allowing the spirit of Satan to gain ascendancy again in our lives.

Jesus has won the victory for us, but we must appropriate it, maintaining a daily holy walk with the Lord. We cannot do this in our own strength, only in the strength which the Holy Spirit gives. In this way we will know true joy and peace in our hearts.

When people enter our home, they should sense peace, the peace of the Holy Spirit in it. Where there is that peace, there is little opportunity for Satan to manifest his hatred and disruptive tactics.

SELF CONTROL

Some people come for deliverance from gluttony or smoking addiction, but they overlook the fact that God has given them the power of self control which they need to exercise before they can be delivered. Sometimes it is merely a matter of them exercising self control because there is no demonic activity involved. We find this set out in the following scripture:

> "*For God has not given us a spirit of fear, but of power and of love and of a sound mind.*" (*self control*) (2 Tim. 1:7).

As Christians, we need to exercise self control at all times. For these reasons the gift of discernment is required to be exercised when we are approached for ministry, because we may well be trying to cast out a demon when the person simply is not exercising God's gift to them, namely the gift of self control.

God has given us sovereignty over our will and we need to exercise our will and walk righteously before God. We must avoid trying to obtain cheap grace from God; we must have sufficient discernment and love to ensure that those who are seeking ministry have indeed crucified the flesh with its lusts.

BALANCE IN WORD

One way in which I personally seek to keep this balance is to take my daily diet of the Word of God from both the Old and New Testaments. I regularly read a portion of scripture each day from the historical books, namely books from Genesis to Job and also read daily from the Psalms and Prophets namely Isaiah through to Malachi.

In the New Testament I regularly read the Gospels and on the same day a portion from the books from Acts to Revelations.

SEVEN

What are Demons?

Demons are spirit beings without bodies. They have an intense desire to live in a body so that they can carry out their own desires and use that body for their own purposes.

"When an unclean spirit goes out of a man, he goes through dry places, seeking rest, and finds none.

"Then he says, 'I will return to my house from which I came.' And when he comes, he finds it empty, swept, and put in order.

"Then he goes and takes with him seven other spirits more wicked than himself, and they enter and dwell there; and the last state of that man is worse than the first. So shall it also be with this wicked generation." (Matt. 12:43-45).

It is clear from this scripture that the demons regard

the body as a house of which they desire to take possession. We also find that demons are not confined to human bodies but will live in animals as well. As we read the story of the demoniac in Mark's Gospel, we find that the demons pass from the man's body to the swine.

> "Now a large herd of swine was feeding there near the mountains.
> And all the demons begged him, saying, 'Send us to the swine, that we may enter them.'
> And at once Jesus gave them permission. Then the unclean spirits went out and entered the swine (there were about two thousand); and the herd ran violently down the steep place into the sea, and drowned in the sea." (Mark 5:11-13).

SEEING A DEMON

In the spirit I have seen demons on many occasions, and on one occasion I saw a demon with my natural eyes. This happened when I was praying in a church with the vicar and he fell under the power of the Holy Spirit. When I looked up, I saw someone standing behind him. The person was eight feet high, with a round white face and clothed in a black garment which stretched out in a triangular fashion to within a few inches of the ground. I commanded this being to leave the building in the name of Jesus the Messiah. The demon began to walk down the aisle and I followed it until it came to the doors of the building. The doors were closed, but it simply disappeared through the doors. I spoke to the vicar subsequently and asked him why he thought it was there. He then remembered that each Wednesday afternoon at 5 p.m., he held a Communion Service in the church and a lady who was an alcoholic would attend the service on her way to the hotel. The Holy Spirit seemed to indicate that this particular demon followed this lady and on this occasion had remained in the church building before it was discerned.

SPIRITS ATTACHED TO PEOPLE

When I am praying with people, I often see in the spirit some spiritual forces attached to their body. For example, if a person suffers from persistent headaches, I often see shapes like darts attached to the back of their neck. Again, on many occasions during the ministry of deliverance, I find that spirit beings in various shapes like fish, or serpents, come out of a person. I frequently see them coming out of the person's mouth. The head appears first, then the stomach and then finally the tail. As I command the demon to go, and it finally goes with its hosts, the person immediately feels lighter, with a complete release from forces of oppression.

Sometimes I see a spirit being standing behind a

person for whom I am praying. It can be a spirit of blackness and, as an hereditary force, it is following the person. It has come down from the ancestors of that person.

Quite frequently these are attached to the base of the person's spine or to their shoulder blade, or to some other part of the body. When the Holy Spirit tells me this and I pass this information on to the person, they often tell me that they have had painful conditions in that particular part of their body.

HOLY SPIRIT THE HELPER

In ministering in the power of the Holy Spirit, I find that He clearly directs me concerning the area of the body for which I should pray. Usually attached to those parts of the body, in the case of sickness, there is some spirit being which can take various shapes and sizes. As I take authority in the name of Jesus the Messiah and command the spirit being to go, then the person knows immediate release and feels the healing power of the Holy Spirit. If I am praying for a woman, I ask her to place her hands first on her own body, the part affected, and then lay my hands on hers and command the spirit to leave. No matter whether it is man, woman or child it is good to lay hands on the part affected and command the spirit to go.

QUENCHING THE HOLY SPIRIT

We should say clearly at this stage that these spirit

beings will quench the power of the Holy Spirit in many cases. Sometimes they appear as spirits of unbelief or as spirits of the occult and unless the person repents and clearly turns from these forces then the anointing of the Holy Spirit will not fall upon that person. As happened to Jesus at Nazareth the Holy Spirit is quenched and the person cannot receive their healing. We must be aware of the need to cast out demons.

COMMISSION OF JESUS

It is noteworthy that Jesus never once sent out His disciples to preach the gospel without also telling them to cast out demons. We find these quotations:

"And when he had called his twelve disciples to him, he gave them power over unclean spirits, to cast them out, and to heal all kinds of sickness and all kinds of disease.

Now the names of the twelve apostles are these: first, Simon, who is called Peter, and Andrew his brother; James the son of Zebedee, and John his brother;

Philip and Bartholomew; Thomas and Matthew the tax collector; James the son of Alphaeus, and Lebbaeus, whose surname was Thaddaeus;

Simon the Canaanite, and Judas Iscariot, who also betrayed him.

These twelve Jesus sent out and commanded them, saying: "Do not go into the way of the Gentiles, and do not enter a city of the Samaritans.

"But go rather to the lost sheep of the house of Israel.

"And as you go, preach, saying, 'The kingdom of heaven is at hand'.

"Heal the sick, cleanse the lepers, raise the dead, cast out demons. Freely you have received, freely give." (Matt. 10:1-8)

Again,

"Then the seventy returned with joy, saying, 'Lord, even the demons are subject to us in your name'." (Luke 10:17

Also,

"Then he appointed twelve, that they might be with him and that he might send them out to preach,
and to have power to heal sicknesses and to cast out demons." (Mark 3:14,15)

Also,

"So they went out and preached that people should repent.
And they cast out many demons, and anointed with oil many who were sick, and healed them."
(Mark 6:12,13)

And again,

"And he said to them, "Go into all the world and preach the gospel to every creature.
"He who believes and is baptized will be saved; but he who does not believe will be condemned.
"And these signs will follow those who believe: In my name they will cast out demons; they will speak with new tongues;
"they will take up serpents; and if they drink anything

deadly, it will by no means hurt them; they will lay hands on the sick, and they will recover." (Mark 16:15-18)

ANGELS OR DEMONS

Demons can be clearly distinguished from angels because angels usually have wings:

"Yes, while I was speaking in prayer, the man Gabriel, whom I had seen in the vision at the beginning, being caused to fly swiftly, reached me about the time of the evening offering." (Daniel 9:21).

Demons do not have wings:

"When an unclean spirit goes out of a man, he goes through dry places, seeking rest, and finds none." (Matt. 12:43).

From the above scripture we also see that angels have bodies of their own. As we have already discussed, demons desire to inhabit a body.

ORIGIN OF DEMONS

Various explanations have been given as to the origin of demons. Some have suggested that they are fallen angels which followed Satan in his rebellion; Others suggest they are the result of intercourse between the "sons of God" referred to in Gen. 6:2, and daughters of men, but whatever their nature we must always remember that they are under a descending order of authority, namely from Satan himself with descending orders of authority, from his generals down to the privates, so to speak. They can acknowledge only Satan as Lord and are in permanent rebellion against God Himself. The great binding force between them is the spirit of fear and domination. They are under the domination of Satan in descending orders of authority and Satan governs them through fear.

It is interesting to note that the Bible describes Satan as Beelzebub or "Lord of the Flies". On occasions I have seen spirits like flies attached to the back of a person's head. When commanded to leave in the name of Jesus the Messiah they come off that person and immediately the person feels free from some kind of oppression.

Frequently people will remark how much lighter they feel after a deliverance has taken place.

EIGHT

How Demons enter

There are a variety of ways and means in which demons can enter people, and I list some of the following:

1. HEREDITARY

The scripture says that the iniquity of the fathers shall be visited on the children "to the third and fourth generation". (Exodus 20:5).

In the occult or other sinful practices, the spirits of sin from the ancestors can enter subsequent generations until there is true repentance and the commanding of that demon to go. That generation can be afflicted even though the person has turned their heart to Jesus Christ. That is why the gift of discernment and deliverance ministry is needed in the body of Christ.

It is important to remember that . . .

"Christ has redeemed us from the curse of the law, having become a curse for us (for it is written, 'Cursed is everyone who hangs on a tree').'' (Galatians 3:13)

It is necessary to appropriate what Jesus has done. People therefore should be encouraged to exercise their will and really believe that they have been delivered from the curse of the law. In this way, authority can be taken over familiar or hereditary spirits which have been following them, but it is necessary for them to exercise their will as these are cut off, and to realize that God has really set them free.

In Chapter 17 we set out an appropriate prayer to be used in such circumstances.

FAITH WALK

Our walk with Jesus Christ is not an intellectual walk, but the walk is an act of faith, and we must appropriate by faith those things which Jesus has already done for us.

2.   DISOBEDIENCE ON THE PART OF PARENTS

Where the parents, particularly the father, do not follow Jesus Christ. In this instance, the home is open to demonic attack and the children can grow up in rebellion. If there is no teaching of the Word in the home, then there are no absolute values, and as the children grow up there is nothing to prevent them entering into all kinds of sexual and other practices which, in turn, bring demons. Parents who encourage their children to smoke or drink can cause them to become addicted to these habits which in turn can become demonic.

3. FRICTION BETWEEN PARENTS

Here again, because the spirit of fear has been allowed to enter into the marriage, young children can be filled with fear and demons of fear can enter them, followed by physical afflictions, such as asthma.

4. MOLESTING OF CHILDREN BY PARENTS

The increasingly common practice of the molesting of children by their fathers allows demon activity to enter. When the child grows old enough to realize what has happened, he or she will often remain unforgiving and this in turn brings in spirits of unforgiveness.

5. FROM THE WOMB

On many occasions, demons enter during pregnancy or at birth. Demons can easily enter a foetus where there is shock, fear or trauma on the part of the mother, particularly where there is disagreement between the parents. I recently prayed for a pastor who had experienced a major problem with violence and lust and the demon which finally manifested clearly entered during pregnancy. The parents were divorced a few years after the child was born but the damage had been done, and the child had carried the spirits of violence and lust through life to middle age before he was delivered.

Spirits of rejection or abortion often enter during pregnancy where the mothers feels rejected or rejects the child. This is particularly true if the mother desires to abort the child.

These spirits can enter the child before birth and remain with it during its life. Once the spirit of rejection has entered it can bring with it many other spirits. This area must often be searched out. It is tremendously helpful when the mother is a believer because when she has repented from the past sin, the act of repentance seems to cut off the demon spirit within the child or young adult. However, whether or not the mother is alive or a believer that demon can still be made to leave by effectual fervent prayer and repentance.

Asking the person to quote from Ephesians 1:6, namely that they are accepted in the beloved and having them really say these words and confess them with their mouth and believe it in their heart can be a tremendous form of deliverance. As they confess these words and believe them, we can then lead them to confess that they accept themselves. This then breaks the hold of rejection.

It is also important to remember the scripture in John's Gospel

"*If you forgive the sins of any, they are forgiven them;
if you retain the sins of any, they are retained.*"
(*John* 20:23)

This scripture has a powerful meaning in this area namely if we retain the sins of others then they will affect us but if we will let them go they will lose their power over us.

These spirits may lay dormant for many years before they finally manifest, but in today's circumstances with a major breakdown of marriages and people living together and bearing children, we must expect a great outpouring of demonic activity among our young people.

6.   THROUGH SIN

We have already mentioned James 1:14, which says:

"*But each one is tempted when he is drawn away by his own desires and enticed.*"
Verse 15:
"*Then, when desire has conceived, it gives birth to sin; and sin, when it is full grown, brings forth death.*"

I have come to believe that behind every sin there is a spirit, and if we continue with the sin then we open ourselves to a spirit. This is true of masturbation, lust, and many other forms of activity which grow to a point of binding us.

Let us listen to what Jesus says:

> "But I say to you that whoever looks at a woman to lust for her has already committed adultery with her in his heart.
>
> "And if your right eye causes you to sin, pluck it out and cast it from you; for it is more profitable for you that one of your members perish, than for your whole body to be cast into hell." (Matt.5:28,29)

We must be very careful that we do not allow spirits to enter through the eye gate, or the ear gate, by allowing our thought life to be out of order. As it becomes out of order, then we allow the spiritual forces to enter. This is why Jesus made the point that simply by looking upon a woman with a desire to commit adultery then we in fact commit adultery in heart. If we allow the spirit of adultery to enter our heart, we have already given ground to the enemy hence we are told by Paul:

> "Casting down arguments and every high thing that exalts itself against the knowledge of God, bringing every thought into captivity to the obedience of Christ." (2 Cor.10:5)

We must keep our thought life and our attitudes pure and yield all our members as instruments of righteousness.

7. SOWING AND REAPING

"Do not be deceived, God is not mocked; for whatever a man sows, that he will also reap.

For he who sows to his flesh will of the flesh reap corruption, but he who sows to the Spirit will of the Spirit reap everlasting life." (Galatians 6:7,8).

This is an inexorable principle of God's laws. Many people are puzzled when they come to Jesus Christ as to why they still have problems with their children. Those problems were sown in the earlier life before the parents came to Jesus Christ and the principle of reaping must be fully worked out. The time of reaping can only be shortened as we yield more and more to Jesus Christ. Demonic activity has often occurred because of the sowing which is taking place and hence the need for discernment and expulsion of the demons.

8. SATAN IS A LEGALIST

Ephesians 4:27 tells us:

"nor give place to the devil".

As we give place to the devil in our lives, he enters and takes over the ground that should be possessed by the Holy Spirit. This is a great cause of demonic activity, hence we should walk holy and justly and without blame before God.

9. OCCULTIC INVOLVEMENT

As we have discussed elsewhere, previous or current occultic involvement on our part or on the part of our previous generations will certainly give entry to demon activities.

10. POSSESSIONS

Sometimes we possess occultic objects in our home, and this is an abomination in the eyes of God:

> "Nor shall you bring an abomination into your house, lest you be doomed to destruction like it; but you shall utterly detest it and utterly abhor it, for it is an accursed thing." (Deut. 7:26)

We should be particularly aware of any eastern objects or carvings with any occultic significance. Similarly, this involvement in any area of the occult such as hypnotism, ouija boards and all the other matters referred to in Appendix 1, can give entry to demonic activity.

11. GENERAL REJECTION

Apart from rejection through parents there can be a sense of general rejection which afflicts people. This can sometimes occur through marriage breakdowns and it requires prayer on the part of the partner who is wronged to bring the other partner back to the Lord. We are told by Jesus to love our enemies, bless those who curse us and do good to those who hate us.

> "But I say to you, love your enemies, bless those

who curse you, do good to those who hate you, and
pray for those who spitefully use you and persecute
you" (Matt. 5:44)

When people pray a blessing for those who have
wronged them by taking away their husband or wife to
live with them then the curse is reversed and God's
love flows into that situation causing confusion on the
part of the spirits involved. As a blessing is prayed for
that person, the spirit of torment, which is coming from
him or her and afflicting the innocent spouse, retires in
confusion and God's Spirit of love comes through the
person who is praying with belief. In this way the spirits
which have caused the breakup of the marriage often
depart and reconciliation takes place.

12. SHOCK

Traumas such as death or the breakdown of marriage, or an accident, can often allow demons to
enter. Satan is no respecter of persons and will take
every opportunity to attack. Frequently I have
found that in the split second just prior to an
accident, the spirit of fear has entered the person,
followed by shock, and then a host of other demon
powers.

In counselling, it is always wise to go back on
any particular trauma which has occurred in a person's life, and it is often found to be the entry point
of demonic activity. In the case of death, where

people not only are subject to grief but kiss or touch dead people, the spirits can be transferred in that way. After prayer for deliverance it is usually good to pray for the healing of the memories.

13. TRANSFERENCE FROM OTHER PEOPLE

It is very easy for demons to be transferred. In the act of sexual intercourse outside of marriage, demonic activity can occur readily as demons are transferred from one body to another. In the case of Christian marriage, this should not occur if both parties are fully committed to Jesus Christ, but where one party is not committed, the other needs to know the sanctifying power of the blood of Jesus in order to retain protection in those circumstances.

14. A DOMINATING PERSONALITY

In a business or church, or similar situations, a dominating personality will often cause a spirit to be transferred to other people. Sometimes we find that subordinates to a person in authority, whether it be in a business or church, will dress alike and look alike in order to ape the person in charge. It often takes the form of having the same type of haircut etc., and wearing the same type of clothes. This opens these people to a transference of spirits from those whom they are copying.

Again, when we are ministering in the deliverance ministry, we need to know the authority of Jesus in our life, otherwise demons may seek to enter us from the person to whom we are ministering. If they do attack us, then we need to know the authority of Jesus in order to resist them. In particular, this means keeping a wholesome mind when we are ministering to persons of the other sex.

When we are doing so always ensure that there is another person of that sex with you. A man should never minister alone to a woman, or vice versa.

Again, a woman or man may be subject to a matriarchial spirit from their mother or a patriarchial spirit from their father as a result of an unhealthy domination by either of the parents over their children. We will be discussing this later in this book.

15. THROUGH ENTERING BUILDINGS

Sometimes a building has been used for immoral purposes, or some evil action, and I have seen cases where children have entered such a place, or even adults, and they have been attacked by demons without realizing it. Their personality has changed and they have needed deliverance.

I well recall a woman coming to me in New Zealand who had gone through a place known as

"The Buried Village" near Tarawera. This had been a Maori village prior to an eruption which overwhelmed it. It had been excavated and she can remember the exact day and time when she was walking through the village and suddenly became an asthmatic. She did not know what had happened to her until many years later when she came for ministry to us. Asthma had entered her. Knowing where it had happened, we were able to identify the problem and deal with the spirit of asthma.

16. OBSESSION

This can become a very powerful demon.

I have found this to be so. I can recall on one occasion praying for a man during a very lengthy deliverance. Finally the Holy Spirit revealed that he had a demon of obsession to which were attached many other demons. It had entered him at the age of 14, when he was at boarding school. He had been wrongly accused one night and all the boys in the dormitory turned on him and accused him. He wept himself to sleep. At that time a spirit of rejection entered him and finally it became an obsession.

I found that as the power of the Holy Spirit came upon me and I pointed at him he would literally somersault in the air. The Holy Spirit indicated that a demon was attached to the man's leg or neck, or other part of the body, and as I pointed at him from a distance, he left the floor and either somersaulted or twisted violently in the air as the spirit left him. It was one of the most powerful demonstrations I have ever seen of the power of the Holy Spirit operating through me. As these demons came out, the noise was positively frightening, until we finally came to the demon of obsession and he left with a loud noise.

17. CURSES

Curses can result in major demonic activity and it can affect generations of families. Dr. Derek Prince in his extremely able teachings in this area suggests that the following conditions can indicate curses, based upon his own wide experience.

1) Mental and emotional breakdown.
2) Repeated or chronic sicknesses (especially without clear medical diagnosis).
3) Repeated miscarriages or related female problems.
4) Breakdown of marriage — family alienation.
5) Continuing financial insufficiency (especially where the income appears sufficient).
6) Accident prone people.

You can clearly see from scripture that there are several sources of curses as follows:—

1) From God himself. For example Deuteronomy

Chapter 27:15 to 26 there are 12 curses pronounced for the breaking of the law of Moses. Some of the curses referred to in these verses are against those who make carved images, who treat their father or mother with contempt, who move their neighbour's landmark, who make the blind to wander off the road, who perverts justice due to the stranger, fatherless and widow, who lies with his father's wife, who lies for sexual purposes with any kind of animal, who lies for sexual purposes with his sister, daughter of his father or the daughter of his mother, who lies for sexual purposes with his mother-in-law, who attacks his neighbour secretly, takes a bribe to slay an innocent person and does not conform to all the Words of this Law.

In Genesis Chapter 12:3 it promises that he will curse those who curse Abraham and bless those who bless Abraham and his descendants. Obviously those who practice anti-semitism invoke God's curse upon themselves.

2) Men can pronounce curses on God's behalf. For example in Joshua Chapter 6:26 Joshua said the following:—

> "Cursed be the man before the Lord who rises up and builds this city Jericho; he shall lay its foundation with his first-born, and with his youngest he shall set up its gates."

This curse was fulfilled as follows:—

> "*In his days Hiel of Bethel built Jericho. He laid its foundation with Abiram his first-born, and with his youngest son Segub he set up its gates, according to the word of the Lord, which he had spoken through Joshua the son of Nun*". (1 *Kings* 16:34).

3) The persons who have authority over us can pronounce curses upon us. Jacob did so when Laban was looking for his gods among the possessions of Jacob. Jacob pronounced a curse on whomever had those gods. (Genesis 31:32)

Jacob was in fact pronouncing a curse on Rachel who died in childbirth. (Genesis 35:16)

We can impose curses upon ourselves.

An example is clearly seen at the crucifixion of Jesus Christ when the leaders of the Jews cursed their own people.

> "*And all the people answered and said, 'His blood be on us and on our chilidren.*'" (*Mathew* 27:25)

INFLUENCES FROM SATAN

There can be satanic instances operating in our life and as part of the process of overcoming these we should resist the devil and bless the place of cursing.

> "*Bless those who persecute you; bless and do not curse.*" (*Romans* 12:14).

Sometimes when people are abusing or cursing us,

it is as a result of demonic activity and can affect us emotionally as well as spiritually. Our answer is to follow the scripture set out above.

In addition we have the example and scripture of professional cursing by professional prophets of Satan. There is a considerable amount of this type of activity going on today, especially with witches covens and other similar types of satanic activity. I have heard of groups praying and fasting against Christian works. They have been praying to Satan or to Lucifer and fasting in order to break the power of these Christian activities. In addition Satan sometimes, through his servants, places or attempts to place curses on God's leaders.

We recall from scripture that Balak, king of the Moabites sent messsengers to Balaam in order to ask him to come and curse the people of Israel. This is set out in Numbers Chapter 22:6. This is an example of the servants of Satan seeking to place a curse over God's people.

The remedies for these situations are set out in Chapter 17 of this book.

NINE

The Personality of Demons

1. THEY HAVE KNOWLEDGE

> "Now there was a man in their synagogue with an unclean spirit. And he cried out, saying, 'Let us alone! What have we to do with you, Jesus of Nazareth? Did you come to destroy us? I know who you are — the Holy One of God!" (Mark 1:23,24)

> "And the evil spirit answered and said, "Jesus I know, and Paul I know; but who are you?" (Acts 19:15)

Recently I prayed with a young man who fell to the floor and voices began to speak out of him. They said, "Why do you hate us?" I pointed out that the Psalmist hates demons with a holy hatred (Psalm 139:22). After a time I realized we were getting nowhere and I told the young man to stand up. At that point, somebody stated that the young man was not a Christian but a Mormon. I realized I had been trying to deal with the Moroni demon of Mormonism so I told the young man that he must be converted and come to Jesus Christ before he could be delivered.

At a subsequent meeting, the same young man came forward. As he approached me, his face twisted, his eyes lit up, and the same voice as previously spoke out of him and said, "So we meet again, preacher!" Friends of the young man told me that since the previous meeting he had come to Jesus Christ and had been water-baptized, but the demon had still not left him. Following further prayer, real signs of deliverance began to occur. The point, however, is that the demon clearly recognized me and knew me.

2. THEY HAVE EMOTION

> "You believe that there is one God. You do well. Even the demons believe — and tremble!" (James 2:19)

Quite frequently when I pray for people I command the demons to tremble in the name of Jesus and the person will go into violent trembling. This is often one of the stands I take in deliverance to ensure that the demon knows that I understand that I have authority in Jesus' name over demons.

3. THEY HAVE A WILL

> "Then he says, 'I will return to my house from which I came.' And when he comes, he finds it empty, swept, and put in order." (Matt.12:44)

"Now a large herd of swine was feeding there near the mountains. And all the demons begged him, saying, 'Send us to the swine, that we may enter them.' And at once Jesus gave them permission. Then the unclean spirits went out and entered the swine (there were about two thousand); and the herd ran violently down the steep place into the sea, and drowned in the sea." (Mark 5:11-13)

In many deliverance sessions, I have come across demons who have known me as an individual and have named me. On one particular occasion, a girl who had been tormented by demons for some time and with whom we had prayed without obtaining full deliverance was woken early one morning. The demon voice spoke to her clearly saying, "I am the demon whom Bill Sub-ritzky tried to get out of you three years ago. I must now leave." The demon voice became so loud that she had to call me for special prayer. The reason why the demons were leaving was that this girl had been under the domination of her mother who had not believed Christians could have a demon. As long as the mother lived in the same home as the daughter and the daughter was under her influence, no deliverance could take place, but when the mother left the home to live elsewhere the demon knew it had to leave as well.

I have found that throughout deliverance sessions I must keep my mind totally centred on Jesus Christ. If my thoughts are diverted and I begin to think of other things, such as further appointments, I frequently find that the demon will speak out and say that it does not have to go because it knows I have another appointment, or that I am too distracted to complete the deliverance.

In Chapter 15 I discuss the case of a Spirit-filled believer to whom deliverance was being administered and the demons said they knew some of the persons who were doing the ministering did not really believe the Word of God in their heart.

We must always remember that greater is He in us than he who is in the world . . .

"... *because he who is in you is greater than he who is in the world.*" (1 John 4:4)

It is clear that the demons can exercise their will. I was recently praying with a person when the demon gave its name as Keysia and it became clear that it was the doorkeeper as well as the "pimp" i.e. telling on others. Whenever, through the Holy Spirit, I named a demon, this particular spirit would say, "Yes, he is here, he is here." I soon concluded that this demon knew the names of the other demons and that he was the doorkeeper, letting the other demons in and out. Having understood this, it made deliverance for that person so much easier.

4. THEY KNOW WHO THEY ARE

"*Then he asked him, 'What is your name?' And he*

answered, saying, 'My name is Legion; for we are many."
(Mark 5:9)

On this occasion they knew their name was Legion. Many times I have found that demons will name themselves giving such names as Anger, Hate, Envy, Jealousy, Fear. They certainly are aware who they are.

Recently in a New Zealand city, I was ministering after a meeting and a lady came to me complaining of a longstanding condition in her stomach. The Holy Spirit clearly told me to stand behind the lady and command the other personality to leave her. The moment that I did so, a deep male voice screamed out of her, "No, I won't go, this is my home . . . I will not leave her!"

I questioned the demon and asked his name, and he said, "My name is Legion". As a number of us prayed together and took authority over this demon, he left her with a violent noise and she was set completely free. At the same time her body was healed as the spirit of sickness left her.

5. THEY ARE UNABLE TO RESPOND TO THE GOSPEL FOR THEIR CONSCIENCE IS TOO SEARED

"Now the Spirit expressly says that in latter times some will depart from the faith, giving heed to deceiving spirits and doctrines of demons, speaking lies in hypocrisy, having their own conscience seared with a hot iron." (1 Timothy 4:1)

Having made Satan their lord and master, they cannot respond to the gospel as their conscience has become too hardened.

6. THEY CAN SPEAK

Demons have an ability to speak and for this purpose they will use a person's voice. Sometimes their voice comes out as a high pitched voice or a scream or a gabble, or sometimes they will speak in a demonic tongue. I have seen all these forms of manifestations. In the case of the demonic tongue, they appear to take over the person and the person seems to go into a trance and it is clear that the person is not speaking in a Holy Spirit tongue.

Whatever the circumstances, I always command the demon to be quiet in those cases and to speak only as I direct. I do not conduct lengthy conversations with demons as a matter of practice, although on occasions I have learned something of value. On the whole, however, it is dangerous to conduct conversations with demons because, not only are they liars, but they will seek to deceive at every opportunity.

On one occasion I prayed with a girl who had been subjected to demon power for a considerable time. Although she was a Spirit-filled Christian seeking to lead a life of holiness, I found that it was difficult to stop the demon from speaking. The girl herself remarked that she was afraid to go into shops on occasions because this voice would take over and begin to speak out of her. Following a lengthy session, she was delivered from this particular demon.

The following scriptures make it clear that the demons have the ability to speak:—

"... Let us alone! What have we to do with you, Jesus of Nazareth? Did you come to destroy us? I know who you are — the Holy One of God!" (Mark 1:24)

Again,

"And he cried out with a loud voice and said, "What have I to do with you, Jesus, Son of the Most High God? I implore you by God that you do not torment me."

For he said to him, "Come out of the man, unclean spirit!"

Then he asked him, "What is your name?" And he answered, saying, "My name is Legion; for we are many."

And he begged him earnestly that he would not send them out of the country.

Now a large herd of swine was feeding there near the mountains.

And all the demons begged him, saying, "Send us to the swine, that we may enter them." (Mark 5:7-12)

Also,

"And the evil spirit answered and said, "Jesus I know, and Paul I know; but who are you?" (Acts 19:15)

Thus demons can speak using the person's voice as a channel.

TEN

Behaviour of Demons

1. THEY SEEK TO ENSLAVE US.

> "For you did not receive the spirit of bondage again to fear, but you received the Spirit of adoption by whom we cry out, "Abba, Father." (Romans 8:15)

Just at they themselves are under the enslaving control of their master, Satan, so in turn they seek to bind us with fear, envy, jealousy and other emotions. Just as they are bond slaves to sin, so they seek to enslave us similarly.

2. THEY TORMENT.

> "For God has not given us a spirit of fear, but of power and of love and of a sound mind." (Self control) (2 Tim. 1:7)

We can also be tormented by failure to accept ourselves. Here again, Satan seeks to deceive us.

3. THEY DECEIVE.

A further one of his characteristics through demons is to deceive:

> "Now the Spirit expressly says that in latter times some will depart from the faith, giving heed to deceiving spirits and doctrines of demons,
> speaking lies in hypocrisy, having their own conscience seared with a hot iron," (1 Tim. 4:1,2).

These deceiving demons seek to tell us that we are not loved by God and not accepted, which of course is contrary to Ephesians 1:6:

> "To the praise of the glory of his grace, by which he has made us accepted in the Beloved."

In the world today, there are many doctrines contrary to the Word of God and it is quite easy to see how so many deceiving spirits are leading well meaning people away from the truth of the gospel. Such doctrines as Christian Science, Amstrongism, Mormonism and similar doctrines, are evidence of the deceiving spirits in the world.

Similarly, many people are misled by spirits from Eastern religions which would encourage them into wrong fasting or abstaining from meats, as Paul says in the same scripture.

> "Forbidding to marry, and commanding to abstain from foods which God created to be received with thanksgiving by those who believe and know the truth."
> (1 Tim. 4:3)

4. THEY ENTICE.

> "*But each one is tempted when he is drawn away by his own desires and enticed.*" (James 1:14)

We must note here that it is our own lust which we allow to entice us away. When our thought life is not right and we allow wrong thoughts to enter, especially lustful ones, then the spirit of lust can follow and draw us away from the things of God. In due time, other spirits also enter as we allow lust to take over.

5. THEY DRIVE AND COMPEL US.

> "*For he had commanded the unclean spirit to come out of the man. For it had often seized him, and he was kept under guard, bound with chains and shackles; and he broke the bonds and was driven by the demon into the wilderness.*" (Luke 8:29)

One of the great characteristics of demon activity is this ability to drive and compel people. Some people find they are doing things which they hate and despite the best endeavours on their part they still are unable to give up certain habits. For example the habits of masturbation or addiction to smoking, or alcohol, or similar unclean habits where the person feels compelled to do these things, even contrary to his own will, can be evidence of demon activity. Lust is a particularly good example of this, where men or women lust after other people's bodies, despite the fact that within them their own conscience is saying that it is wrong. Something seems to take them over in those circumstances.

Similarly, demons of murder and assault are often present and we find people who have committed such crimes saying afterwards that they don't know why they did it. This can often be the result of demon activity.

6. THEY DEFILE

> "To the pure all things are pure, but to those who are defiled and unbelieving nothing is pure; but even their mind and conscience are defiled." (Titus 1:15)

I have attended Rock Festivals as a speaker, leading large groups of Christians. We have observed, at these Rock Festivals, where many tens of thousands of people have been gathered in the one area, the defiling of the human body. At one such festival, nearly one-third of the persons present were stark naked and many of them were covering themselves with mud from head to foot. Others were defiling themselves by bowing down to Buddhas, whilst others lay on the ground stark naked as there was an incantation made by an eastern priest encouraging the demons to enter their bodies. As they did so, the people grunted like pigs. We were told this was a form of spiritual rebirth.

At yet another Rock Festival, teenagers were diving through the toilet seats into the excreta and beginning to drown before they were pulled out by their feet. Yes,

Satan wants to defile at every level and he will do so at the very first opportunity.

7. DEMONS CAUSE FRICTION BETWEEN PEOPLE AND FIGHT AGAINST PEACE IN EVERY WAY.

The great characteristic of demon activity is *restlessness*. Demons fight against a person's inner harmony as well as their peace of mind and physical wellbeing. The result is that people find that their relationships with other people, especially their closest relatives and friends is often in jeopardy. One of the most marked activities of demons is to cause friction betwen those who should be in harmony, especially husband and wife. Their whole activity is against harmony.

We remember that in John 14:27. Jesus said:

"Peace I leave with you, my peace I give to you; not as the world gives do I give to you. Let not your heart be troubled, neither let it be afraid."

Similarly, in Matthew 10:13, Jesus referred to the peace which the twelve apostles would bring as they entered households:

"If the household is worthy, let your peace come upon it. But if it is not worthy, let your peace return to you."

The opposite of peace is disharmony, and this is where Satan's kingdom reigns supreme.

In the same way, we may find great difficulty in having a harmonious relationship with those around us or in our external circumstances. If we find there is a lack of peace around us, and with those with whom we deal, then this can be a mark of demonic activity.

Just watch a person who is always restless. You will find that there is no peace within them, they are always up and going and can never settle down. That person, in later life, may manifest such conditions as arthritis, heart attacks or asthma and the like. They can never sit still for more than a few moments and certainly have little time to listen to others.

While one cannot be adamant in every case and say that these people are subject to demon activity, there is a very great likelihood that in fact this is their problem.

I am indebted to Dr. Derek Prince for his exposition of the psychological and physical aspects of demon activity, and I set them out as follows:

(1) PSYCHOLOGICAL

a. Persistent or recurrent evil or destructive emotions or attitudes dominate a person even contrary to his own will or nature, e.g., resentment, hatred, fear, envy, jealousy, pride, self-pity, tension, impatience.

b. "Moods" . . . unreasonable, sudden, extreme fluctuations, e.g., from talkative exhilaration to taciturn depression. A typical example of such a situation is where we do not know how the person will react to us at a particular time. One moment they will be all right, but the next moment they will have a reaction which we cannot fathom.

c. Various forms of religious error or bondage, e.g., submission to unscriptural doctrine or prohibitions, unnatural asceticism, refusal to eat normal foods, superstitious observances of all kinds, all forms of idolatry.

d. Resort to charms, fortune telling, astrology, mediums, etc.

e. Enslaving habits, e.g., gluttony, alcohol, nicotine, drugs, sexual immorality or perversion of all kinds, uncontrollable unclean thoughts or looks.

f. Blasphemy, mockery, unclean language.

g. Persistent or violent opposition to the truth of scripture of the work of the Holy Spirit.

(2) PHYSICAL

a. Unnatural restlessness and talkativeness, muttering.

b. The eyes glazed or unnaturally bright and protruding, or unable to focus naturally.

c. Froth at the mouth, fetid breath.

d. Palpitation or unnaturally exhilarated action of the heart.

e. Shunning, recoiling from, or fighting against the power of the Holy Spirit.

In many cases, one of the foregoing symptoms alone would not be conclusive indication of demon presence or activity, but where several of the symptoms are found together, the probability of demon activity is extremely high.

DEMONS SEEK TO OPPRESS US

As we read earlier in Acts 10:38, God anointed Jesus of Nazareth with the Holy Spirit and with power who went about doing good and healing all who were OPPRESSED by the devil, for God was with Him.

When people have demons within them they will often oppress people who surround them, besides feeling oppressed themselves. The great desire of demons is to control others. Sometimes when we enter a building, or are with a person and sense an oppression around them. This spirit of oppression will seek to attack us and bring us into bondage. As an example of this, I find that when I have an employee and I am afraid of asking him to do something then that person is no longer of any use to me unless he will repent. In other words, the spirit within him seeks to control me and make me afraid to ask him to do something. Once a person reaches this point, then he is of little use as an employee unless he repents. Of course, if he will not turn to Jesus Christ and repent, there is little that one can do about the situation. If that person is allowed to continue working for you, then after a while the spirit within him will increasingly control you because you are afraid to ask the person to do the things you want him to do as an employee.

Many times I pray with a person and, although there is no manifestation of the departure of demons, they will suddenly say, "Oh, I feel much lighter!" or, "Something heavy has left me". Again, when praying for a person who has a demon, we find that sometimes that person becomes very heavy, as though weighed down. It is almost impossible to hold them up because the demon seems to make their body so heavy that the only thing to do is to let them sink to the ground. I usually prevent this by getting several people to hold the person up and, when the demon leaves, suddenly the person is lighter. We must be able to discern whether a person is really being "slain" by the Holy Spirit or whether a demon is taking that person to the ground in order to hide and give the impression that, in fact, the person has been slain in the Holy Spirit. Oppression can be an actual physical manifestation as well as a spiritual manifestation.

DEMONS OPERATE IN TWO WAYS
(1) From outside of the body.

In this case we must resist them:

> "*Therefore submit to God. Resist the devil and he will flee from you.*" (James 4:7)

> "*Be sober, be vigilant; because your adversary the devil walks about like a roaring lion, seeking whom he may devour.*
> *Resist him, steadfast in the faith, knowing that the same sufferings are experienced by your brotherhood in the world.*" (1 Peter 5:8,9)

We must learn to be able to resist the devil. This will come from our knowledge of Jesus Christ, belief in Him, and the authority which He has given us.

(2) Alternatively, demons can operate within the body, in which case we must expel them:

> "When evening had come, they brought to him many who were demon-possessed. And he cast out the spirits with a word, and healed all who were sick." (Matt. 8:16)

> "And he was preaching in their synagogues throughout Galilee, and cast out demons." (Mark 1:39)

One way in which I find immediate release in the case of demons within people is to encourage them to breathe in the Holy Spirit and breathe out sharply. If they will do this say four or five times, they will find that the demon has left them as it has been expelled from their body and the Holy Spirit has refilled them.

ELEVEN

Principal Areas of Demon Activity

1. IN OUR ATTITUDES, EMOTIONS AND RELATIONSHIPS.

We must remember that the Bible describes us as being spirit, soul and body.

> "Now may the God of peace himself sanctify you completely; and may your whole spirit, soul, and body be preserved blameless at the coming of our Lord Jesus Christ."
> (1 Thess. 5:23)

Here we have a clear definition of spirit, soul and body, and Satan will attack these three areas.

In the areas of our emotions and relationships we find that Satan seeks to place bondages upon us, especially in the area of our relationships. Thus we find spirits of fear, resentment, hatred and rebellion entering into our emotional lives if we permit them to do so. This can happen particularly in regard to relationships with other people, especially those closest to us.

Let us remember that Jesus described Satan as a murderer from the beginning and a liar and the father of lies.

PARENTS

Where we fail to honour our parents,

> "Honour your father and mother," which is the first commandment with a promise:
> "That it may be well with you and you may live long on the earth." (Ephesians 6:2,3)

God has promised to curse us if we do not do these things:

> "Cursed is the one who treats his father or his mother with contempt.' And all the people shall say, 'Amen!'" (Deut 27:16)

Here again, demonic powers enter us if we fail to honour our parents.

Something that is intended to be a blessing from God, which we should receive after we honour our father and mother becomes a curse when we dishonour our parents, with the result that many people do not have things well with them and they do not live long upon the earth.

OTHER RELATIONSHIPS

In the ministry of counselling and deliverance, I always turn to relationships in the first instance and check out the person's relationships with their parents as well as other relatives, then any other person. It is through this area of relationships that Satan enters the door, if our relationships are not in accordance with the scriptures.

Where there are wrong relationships between husband and wife, and where husbands do not obey the scripture, e.g.,

> *"Husbands, love your wives, just as Christ also loved the church and gave himself for it,"*
> *"So husbands ought to love their own wives as their own bodies; he who loves his wife loves himself."* (Ephesians 5:25 & 28)

These areas of wrong relationships and attitudes can cause torment and allow disharmony to enter.

CHILDREN

I have already made the point that I find many children suffer asthma because of fear which has entered them at an early age in the first place. This fear has come in because of arguments between the parents which the children have overheard and in time that fear has brought the spirit of asthma.

UNFORGIVENESS

The area of unforgiveness, of course, provides a stronghold for Satan's power and as we have already seen in Matthew 18:34, 35, God has promised that the tormentors (that is demons) will come if we do not forgive.

The only part of the Lord's Prayer that is repeated is that dealing with forgiveness. Jesus said in Matthew's Gospel:

> "For if you forgive men their trespasses, your heavenly Father will also forgive you.
> "But if you do not forgive men their trespasses, neither will your Father forgive your trespasses." (Matt. 6:14,15)

The area of unforgiveness provides a powerful entry point for Satan.

2. THOUGHTS OF THE MIND

Here again the mind is part of the soulish area and Satan will attack with thoughts of doubt, unbelief, compromise, indecision and procrastination.

When I attended Law School at University, I was told that one of the main objectives of the course was to make me think for myself and to be independent of mind. While this is commendable as a natural objective, it can lead to problems when we move in the spiritual realm because our natural mind is against God.

> "Because the carnal mind is enmity against God; for it is not subject to the law of God, nor indeed can it be." (Romans 8:7)

RENEWED MIND

Until our mind is renewed by the Spirit of Christ and

made subject to the Holy Spirit it can remain in rebellion against God's Word. Accordingly, we find that the spirit of "blockage of mind", or doubt, unless cast out or renounced can often prevent a person from seeking the baptism of the Holy Spirit and speaking in tongues.

Satan seeks at every opportunity to bring thoughts of doubt and unbelief into our mind. That is why the scriptures tell us that we must bring every thought into captivity to Jesus Christ.

> *"Casting down arguments and every high thing that exhalts itself against the knowledge of God, bringing every thought into captivity to the obedience of Christ,"* (2 *Cor.* 10:5)

UNCLEAN THOUGHTS

A carnal mind is also a breeding ground for unclean thoughts. As we read pornographic books or allow wrong thoughts to enter our mind through our eyes, which are commonly called "the eye gate", or our ears, commonly called "the ear gate", then these can take hold in our mind and cause us to enter into habits which are unclean. In the same way, masturbation, while it may start as an innocent activity, conjures up thoughts of sexual fantasy until finally the person is caught up in complete bondage in his thought life with the spirit of lust. This in turn can bring in many other spirits.

It is wonderful to be able to pray in the Spirit and speak in tongues when we are under attack in the area of our mind. With the assistance of the Holy Spirit we can then speak past our natural mind direct to God.

3. THE TONGUE

Another area of activity is the TONGUE. Many people tell lies without realizing that they are doing so. In a recent publication it was stated that psychiatrists claim that people tell up to 200 lies a day without knowing that they are doing so. The spirit of lying can rest upon our tongue like the spirit of unclean talk and blasphemy. Many people curse and swear without in fact knowing that they are doing so because the spirit on their tongue automatically causes them to utter filthy words during the course of their ordinary speech. I have often seen the lying, blaspheming, and gossiping spirit on a person's tongue as they are being delivered. In this event, with their permission, I will place my finger on their tongue, or anoint their tongue, and command the spirit to leave as they renouce the unclean or blaspheming spirit.

BAPTISM OF HOLY SPIRIT

It is noteworthy that, when praying for people for the baptism of the Holy Spirit, we often find that a spirit other than the Holy Spirit, rests upon their tongue and they begin to speak in a demonic tongue. Satan has become so accustomed to using that person's tongue for blasphemy or lying, that he often causes a lying or blaspheming spirit to rest on the person's tongue while deliverance is taking place. The Holy Spirit drives out these and other spirits as the person surrenders their tongue to Jesus Christ. As we see the person going into a trance-like attitude and mechanically speaking without realizing what they are doing, then we know that it is indeed a demonic tongue. I usually encourage the person to stop speaking out and to start again with a Holy Spirit tongue. Finally the spirit is driven from that person's tongue. This may need to be done several times in order to obtain complete deliverance. We will always know in our spirit that the person has a liberty in their tongue which is of the Holy Spirit rather than a force which is driving their tongue into some strange language which is not from God.

4. SEX

It must be remembered that demons desire to have a body in which to live. They do not care whether it is the body of a pig, a horse, or your body or mine. A sexual demon requires sexual organs through which to lust, a lying demon needs a tongue for lying or blasphemy. Homosexuality is demonic. If there is real repentance on the part of the person concerned they can be set free.

HOMOSEXUAL DELIVERED

Recently I was privileged to pray with a man who had lived with another man for seven years and they had owned a farm jointly. This man came to me in an Anglican church and said he desired to be free from the demon of homosexuality. There was real repentance on his part. As I prayed for him in front of the congregation, he fell on the floor and wriggled along the floor like a snake, making violent noises. As he reached the back of the church, the demon of homosexuality suddenly left him and he stood up completely free.

Some years ago while in Tonga, a group of islands in the South Pacific, the Holy Spirit indicated by the word of knowledge that there was a man in the audience whose one leg was considerably shorter than the other. I asked the man to come forward, and from the back of the crowd a young man came. His left leg was some four inches shorter than his right leg. It was obvious from his appearance that he was a homosexual and I asked him how long the deformity had been in his leg. He answered, "Seven years". I then asked him how long he had been a homosexual and he said, "Seven years". I told him that if he would renounce the demon of homosexuality and receive Jesus as Saviour, he would be instantly healed. He agreed to do so and immediately after he had renounced the demon of homosexuality and made Jesus his Saviour, I laid hands upon him and his leg came down to the length of the other leg and he was absolutely healed.

AIDS

There is no question in my mind that the current

plague of AIDS (Acquired Immunity Deficiency Syndrome) which is killing so many homosexuals is exactly the penalty described in Romans 1:27

> *"Likewise also the men, leaving the natural use of the woman, burned in their lust for one another, men with men committing what is shameful,* AND RECEIVING IN THEMSELVES THE PENALTY OF THEIR ERROR WHICH WAS DUE."

It is noteworthy that this disease appeared amongst homosexuals and not amongst lesbians. We note that in verse 26 of Romans 1, referring to women who become lesbians, it does not include the latter part of verse 27 describing the penalty which homosexuals receive.

As Christians we should love the homosexual but hate the demon of homosexuality. It is wonderful to see people freed from this demon when they really want to be free.

ORAL SEX

Other forms of sexual perversion are demonic. For example, there are various forms of oral sex. I have frequently been approached by women who have tremendous problems, and I have seen this spirit upon them. I have seen a vision of the male sexual organ in front of their mouth. I have asked them whether they have participated in this activity. They have confessed that this is so, and when they have renounced it the demon has left and a spirit of sickness has left them, with vomiting taking place with the manifestations. They have then stood up, completely healed.

MASTURBATION

Similarly, masturbation can become demonic. A sign of its demon activity is when the person concerned cannot give it up, that is, it has become driving and compelling and tormenting.

It is absolutely wrong for Christian teachers to say that masturbation is normal and should be encouraged. I believe this grieves the Holy Spirit in every way because I have, during many years of deliverance ministry, found that people who have been involved in masturbation for any length of time have the utmost difficulty in giving it up; but worse than that, many other demons have entered as they have surrendered themselves to the demon of masturbation.

We must remember that, having created man in His Own Image, as male and female, God saw everything He had made and indeed it was very good. (Genesis 1:31).

Sex within the context of marriage is good, it is part of God's purposes. Satan would seek to take it and twist and pervert it.

The lowest form of sexual perversion is in sex with animals. Here again, we find Satan's purposes fulfilled in defiling what should be the temple of the Holy Spirit.

5. ADDICTIONS

Another main area of demon activity is in addictions. Many people are addicted to smoking or alcohol or over-eating. Sometimes these arise from sheer habit but at other times because of a sense of unworthiness or frustration on their part. I have been privileged to pray on many occasions for people to be delivered from the spirit of smoking.

Where there is true repentance and they desire to be so delivered, I will place my hand on their nose and ask them to breath in and out through their nose. After a short time, a manifestation will begin to take place. I am convinced that the desire for smoking enters through the eyes, that is by persons watching others smoke, because the demon appears to come out of the eyes.

SMOKING ADDICTION

At at recent Rock Festival, in order to gain the attention of a screaming mob, I prayed for several people who were addicted to smoking and, as the demons manifested the crowd became silent. I told them that this was exactly what they had within them, namely demons, and gradually many began to come out in true repentance to seek Jesus Christ and be released from demon power. Quite often we can smell the actual spirit of smoking leaving the person.

At the time of my own conversion, I had an addiction to alcohol although I would not have regarded myself as an alcoholic. I was a social and business drinker. I could not give up alcohol, but when I was converted God changed my bloodstream so as to create an intolerance for alcohol, preventing me from having any quantity of alcohol. I know what it is to be delivered from the spirit of alcohol.

I have been privileged to pray with many people with excessive appetites who have been in a true state of repentance, and where the spirit of gluttony has been involved. While great emphasis is placed on alcohol and its demonic influence, I feel that too little is placed on gluttony. In some Western countries it is appalling to see the physical size of many Christians and it is apparent that their bodies are not God-honouring as temples of the Holy Spirit because of their food intake which can often be the result of gluttony. The answer, of course, is that God has not given us the spirit of fear but of power, of love, and of self control.

"For God has not given us a spirit of fear, but of power and of love and of a sound mind." (Self control) (2 Tim. 1:7)

Where Christians exercise this spirit of God's self control and also the fruit of self control (Gal.5:23) then the demonic power loosens its grip and their appetite comes under control again.

The root of so many of these addictions is frustration. So many people feel frustrated and allow this attitude to develop into a spiritual problem. Frustration is the root, so to speak, and its branches can include addiction. If we deal with the frustration then we deal with the addiction.

The frustration could have entered at childhood or in wrong relationships and until there is real forgiveness manifested on the part of the sufferer there will be no true deliverance.

6. SICKNESS

Another area of demon activity is within our body. Many allergies, heart conditions, arthritic conditions, cancers and similar activities are demonic. The spirit of infirmity can enter and bind a person physically:

"And behold, there was a woman who had a spirit of infirmity eighteen years, and was bent over and could in no way raise herself up." (Luke 13:11)

When Jesus healed this woman from the spirit of infirmity, her physical condition was restored.

During a teaching seminar some time ago, I was encouraging people to understand the anointing of the Holy Spirit. As I asked the Holy Spirit to fall in full power with His anointing, a lady seated in the front row, who had been crippled by a stroke, suddenly fell on the floor under the power of the Holy Spirit. The anointing had broken the yoke and she stood up totally healed from the spirit of stroke.

Similarly, in the Suva Cathedral, Fiji, a man, touched by the power of the Holy Spirit, was instantly healed as the spirit of stroke left him.

Many allergies, such as asthma, hayfever and other conditions can be the result of a spirit of infirmity and when they are cast out the condition of the person instantly improves.

TWELVE

Ways in which Satan operates

HERESIES

Heresies are usually truths taken to extreme so that finally they become a departure from the true Christian faith. Somebody awakens to a particular truth and instead of bringing total balance through the Word of God they major on this particular truth until it becomes out of line with the rest of the Word of God. Finally, in order to sustain their particular argument, increasingly unscriptural points of view are used until in the end the person is in total error. The scriptures are perfectly clear that a false balance is abomination to the Lord:

> "A *false balance is an abomination to the* Lord, *But a just weight is his delight."* (*Proverbs* 11:1)

Again, we find these shall happen in the last days as set out in 1 Timothy:

"Now the Spirit expressly says that in latter times some
will depart from the faith, giving heed to deceiving spirits and
doctrines of demons,
speaking lies in hypocrisy, having their own conscience
seared with a hot iron;" (1 Tim. 4:1,2)

1. JEHOVAH'S WITNESSES

If we take an example, such as Jehovah's Witnesses,
we find that it is impossible to reason with these people.
They have been given a line of scriptures on which they
major and will not listen to any contrary argument. They
have, of course, produced their own Bible and changed
the truths contained in the inspired Word of God in
order to justify their particular heresy. This is the final
stage of heresy.

2. MORMONS

As these particular heresies are persisted with, we
will invariably find that there is a satanic prince behind
that form of doctrine. For example, in the case of the
Mormons, I have found when ministering to these
people that they are in the grip of satanic princes of the
power of the air, such as Moroni and a prince named
Manasseh. Recently, a group of people who had left the
Mormon Church visited my home because they realized
they needed some form of deliverance. As they entered
my home, the Holy Spirit spoke to me and said that they
had brought in the spirit of Manasseh. I felt the hair on my
body rise as I knew that this prince was standing with

them. They were now committed as Christians but there were still certain bondages upon them. They produced a white garment which Mormans wear and which they used in demonstrating the way in which the Mormon Church worked. Immediately the Holy Spirit told me it was to be destroyed, and they agreed to do this. We took the garment outside and burned it, and at that point the spirit of Manasseh disappeared.

3. FREEMASONRY

We must remember that Mormonism has a connection with Freemasonry. The cult of Freemasonry worships heathen gods, Baal and Ashtaroth, and, in the higher orders, Lucifer (Satan). Much of the ritual of Mormonism is connected to Freemasonry. Many innocent people are involved in the Mormon Church because they have no better understanding. We must continue to love them and not judge them. I believe we are to stand against the spirit of Mormonism but love those who are held in its bondage. We must continue to pray against the demon which binds them so that they can be set free.

There is only one way to God the Father and that is through Jesus Christ crucified. Jesus said, "I am the Way, the Truth and the Life; no one comes to the Father except through Me."

Only the Holy Spirit gives us access to the Father:

"For through him we both have access by one Spirit to the Father." (Ephesians 2:18)

When we try to seek access to God through other gods or through other ways, then judgement is brought on succeeding generations:

> "You shall have no other gods before me.
> "You shall not make for yourself any carved image, or any likeness of anything that is in heaven above, or that is in the earth beneath, or that is in the water under the earth;
> "You shall not bow down to them nor serve them. For I, the Lord your God, am a jealous God, visiting the iniquity of the fathers on the children to the third and fourth generations of those who hate me." (Exodus 20:3-5)

Our God is a jealous God and we are not to attempt to worship any other god or idol. This brings judgment upon ourselves and upon our succeeding generations, and for this reason we find many people bound by hereditary spirits.

4. HEREDITARY SPIRITS

Many times when I go to pray with people, the Holy Spirit clearly indicates to me that another spirit surrounds that person and that that spirit is an hereditary spirit which has come down through the generations, sometimes through the father or through the mother. It may have gone back several generations, and the Lord may indicate quite clearly by the Holy Spirit in a particular case that the spirit comes down through the father, and in turn through his grandfather on his mother's side. The Holy Spirit is very specific in these areas.

These hereditary spirits can be idolatry, lust, fear or any other form of spirit, and as they are bound and loosed from the person, deliverance takes place.

5. FOOD

Some people are carried away by various ideas about food, including the idea that they should not eat meat but become vegetarians. This is dealt with in 1 Tim. 4:1-5:

> "Now the Spirit expressly says that in latter times some will depart from the faith, giving heed to deceiving spirits and doctrines of demons,
> speaking lies in hypocrisy, having their own conscience seared with a hot iron,
> forbidding to marry, and commanding to abstain from foods which God created to be received with thanksgiving by those who believe and know the truth.
> For every creature of God is good, and nothing is to be refused if it is received with thanksgiving;
> for it is sanctified by the word of God and prayer."

The early church met in Council at Jerusalem and made it clear that no greater bondages were to be laid upon the Gentiles, than abstaining from meats offered to idols, from blood, from things strangled, and from fornication. They did not need to be circumcised in accordance with the law.

> "For it seemed good to the Holy Spirit, and to us, to lay upon you no greater burden than these necessary things:
> that you abstain from things offered to idols, from blood,

from things strangled, and from sexual immorality. If you keep yourselves from these, you will do well. Farewell. (Acts 15:28,29)

One of the wonderful chapters in the New Testament which gives us a balanced perspective on matters of eating, Sabbath keeping and drinking, is Romans Chapter 14, and it repays deep study.

6. VEGETARIANISM AND MEAT-EATERS

We are told not to enter into disputes over doubtful things:

> *"For one believes he may eat all things, but he who is weak eats only vegetables.*
>
> *Let not him who eats despise him who does not eat, and let not him who does not eat judge him who eats; for God has received him."* (Romans 14:2,3)

7. SABBATH KEEPERS

For those who would demand that we observe a special day above another we find:

> *"One person esteems one day above another; another esteems every day alike. Let each be fully convinced in his own mind.*
>
> *He who observes the day, observes it to the Lord; and he who does not observe the day, to the Lord he does not observe it. He who eats, eats to the Lord, for he gives God thanks; and he who does not eat, to the Lord he does not eat, and gives God thanks.*
>
> *For none of us lives to himself, and no one dies to himself. For if we live, we live to the Lord; and if we die, we die to*

the Lord. Therefore, whether we live or die, we are the Lord's.

For to this end Christ died and rose and lived again, that he might be Lord of both the dead and the living.

But why do you judge your brother? Or why do you show contempt for your brother? For we shall all stand before the judgment seat of Christ."

"Therefore let us not judge one another anymore, but rather resolve this, not to put a stumbling-block or a cause of offence in our brother's way." (Romans 14:5-10&13)

Clearly, we are not to judge one another as to what we eat or what day we keep. We are not to judge one another in this respect. If one person wants to keep Saturday as the Sabbath, then that is fine, but he is not to judge the person who wants to keep Sunday as the Sabbath.

8. FALSE PROPHETS

The prediction that there would be false prophets in the last times is set out in 2 Peter 2:1:

"But there were also false prophets among the people, even as there will be false teachers among you, who will secretly bring in destructive heresies, even denying the Lord who bought them, and bring on themselves swift destruction."

"Little children, it is the last hour; and as you have heard that the antichrist is coming, even now many antichrists have come, by which we know that it is the last hour." (1 John 2:18)

"For false christs and false prophets will rise and show signs and wonders to deceive, if possible, even the elect." (Mark 13:22)

"They went out from us, but they were not of us; for if they had been of us, they would have continued with us; but they went out that they might be made manifest, that none of them were of us.

But you have an anointing from the Holy One, and you know all things.

I have not written to you because you do not know the truth, but because you know it, and that no lie is of the truth. Who is a liar but he who denies that Jesus is the Christ? He is antichrist who denies the Father and the Son." (1 John 2:19-22)

"Beloved, do not believe every spirit, but test the spirits, whether they are of God; because many false prophets have gone out into the world.

By this you know the Spirit of God: Every spirit that confesses that Jesus Christ has come in the flesh is of God, and every spirit that does not confess that Jesus Christ has come in the flesh is not of God. And this is the spirit of the antichrist, which you have heard was coming, and is now already in the world." (1 John 4:1-3)

9. FALSE RELIGIONS

There are many voices in the world today and they seek to deny the diety of Jesus Christ. Jesus said:

"...I am the way, the truth, and the life. No one comes to the Father except through me." (John 14:6)

We can only come to the Father through Jesus crucified. Similarly, we can have access to the Father by only one Holy Spirit.

> *"For through him we both have access by one spirit to the Father."* (Eph. 2:18)

ANOINTED ONE

When preaching in India recently, I found it necessary to keep emphasizing that Jesus was the Messiah, the Anointed One, the only Son of God. The people there knew of Jesus but regarded Him as a prophet or a teacher, but not as the Anointed One. As I continued preaching Jesus the Anointed One, the Messiah, demons began to manifest, and great healings took place as people believed the message.

The sins of one generation are visited on the following generations up to the fourth generation. As a result, if our parents have gone under another spirit, this spirit will flow down through the generations and will follow us. That is why it must be repented from and we must forgive our ancestors even though we have turned to Jesus Christ. This spirit will manifest itself as a spirit of deception and will seek to take away the truth that Jesus is the only way, the truth and the life. It will seek to show other ways of approaching God. Until it is totally repented from, it will retain a hold over our lives.

For example, I have already remarked on the spirit of Freemasonry. Again I have prayed with many people who have a Hindu background and very frequently the spirit of monkey god will still manifest on them, even though they have turned their hearts to Jesus Christ. Until that demon is commanded to leave them and they repent of it, the spirit will still seek to be attached to them.

DEMON OF ANGER

Now the spirit which rises up when we begin to expose the spirit of heresy is the demon of anger. It is noteworthy that, whenever we begin to point out an unbalanced doctrine, particularly one which "tickles the ears" of the believers, then the spirit of anger manifests on the part of the person who is bound by the heresy. They are not prepared to listen because the demon of deception within them is not prepared to listen to the whole truth:

> "For the time will come when they will not endure sound doctrine, but according to their own desires, because they have itching ears, they will heap up for themselves teachers;
>
> and they will turn their ears away from the truth, and be turned aside to fables." (2 Tim.4:3,4)

I find that, often related to the demon of anger, is the demon of obsession and this manifests in people who are involved in heresy.

People desire to hear the good things of life and shrink from the way of the cross with its tribulations. The

Christian life has its testing and tribulations and we cannot escape them if we are following the way of the Cross.

> "... *We must through many tribulations enter the kingdom of God.*" (Act 14:22)

10. ROCK MUSIC

One has only to be present at Rock Festivals to realize the spirit of violence and hatred which can come through many forms of rock music today. We remember that the term "Rock and Roll" has its origins in the sexual act and the beat of the rock music draws the demon powers. Satan himself loves music and as we recall, he was the Anointed Cherub created by God and involved with timbrels and pipes which signify music:

> "*You were in Eden, the garden of God; Every precious stone was your covering: The sardius, topaz, and diamond, beryl, onyx and jasper, sapphire, turquoise, and emerald with gold. The workmanship of your timbrels and pipes was prepared for you on the day you were created.*
>
> *You were the anointed cherub who covers; I established you; You were on the holy mountains of God; You walked back and forth in the midst of fiery stones.*
>
> *You were perfect in your ways from the day you were created, till iniquity was found in you.*" (Ezek. 28:13-15)

In a greater measure, day by day, we are finding spirits of Antichrist manifesting themselves. For example in rock music, by using "back masking" techniques.

Satan manifests himself in this way and we have discovered that in the records there are such statements coming through at a sublimal level as "Satan is God ... Murder ... Suicide", and other demonic words and phrases.

I can well recall a time with I was speaking in an Anglican Church in New Zealand and, following the service, was ministering to those who were waiting. A young man came forward and indicated that there was strife in his marriage. The Holy Spirit told me that the young man had been listening to the record called "Jonathan Livingstone Seagull". I asked him if this was so and he replied that this was correct. I told him he would need to renouce this music because it was given by demons and those who had received the music and lyrics had confirmed in writing that they had heard these demon voices giving them this music. As the young man renounced the spirit of "Jonathan Livingstone Seagull" in the name of Jesus the Messiah, he raised his hands horizontally with his body and flapped them like wings. At the same time, to the astonishment of all assembled, out of his mouth came the squawk of a seagull as the demon left him. Needless to say, his marriage was healed after the demon power had gone from his home. It was necessary to counsel him to break all those records.

Today, through the medium of rock music and eastern religion, much heresy is entering our homes and we must stand against it.

Thus Satan was involved in the music in God's temple before he fell from grace.

SPIRIT OF PRIDE

One of the great dangers in music is the spirit of pride which enters. We must always watch that we worship God and not the spirit of music. There is a great danger that the spirit of music and the worship of music itself as well as perfection of music may enter choirs. It can easily be discerned. A spirit of pride seems to come as the music itself is worshipped rather than the Lord.

During the years, I have found that one of the greatest hindrances to the move of the Holy Spirit can be a choir in a church. The choir members may have resisted the move of the Holy Spirit. This is not in all cases, but in many cases I have noted this. It seems as though, in seeking perfection in singing and in worship of the spirit of music, an ability has been lost to know the anointing of God.

On many records today we find that if they are played backwards, we can hear voices encouraging us to worship Satan, or to commit suicide, or violence, rape, or some similar crime. These voices cannot be heard at the normal hearing level when the music is being played but it is just below that level so that it is the subliminal advertising. Some rock bands are noted for the amount of violence that they can create as they bring the spirit of violence into their festivals. We must be very careful that the music we listen to edifies both our spirit and the Spirit of the Living God, rather than the sensual areas of our emotions which stir up desires that are not of God. One has only to look at the record covers of many rock bands to realize that demon worship is involved. Rock music and drugs often go together, with the resultant demonic activity.

SOWING AND REAPING

We reap what we have sown. If we have been ignorant of these matters and have brought up our children in the way of the world whereby they worship these forms of rock music, then we will find that, when we come to Jesus Christ as personal Saviour and commit our lives to Him, there is a great need for repentance on our part in these areas. As we continue to pray for our children and bind the demon powers which may still be in our homes because of the playing of such music, we can ask for G﹍ '' love to flow into that situation. As our children begin ﹍ see God's love flowing through us, they will respond and gradually the desire for such forms of music will depart.

Many parents who have come to Jesus Christ realize that rock music is wrong and must exercise great wisdom in these circumstances. If they seek to shut it out immediately from their home, they are in danger of causing their children to leave home, and they must seek the Spirit of the Living God and His wisdom in how to cope with these situations. Usually if God's love is manifested and the demon powers are bound, then we find that the desire for such music departs.

When there is true repentance from such music on the part of all concerned, records must be destroyed and all trace of them removed from the home as demon powers can still be attached to them.

DANCING

One of the most frightening cases in which I was ever involved was a case where a woman had watched a form of hula dancing in the Cook Islands in the South Pacific. She was a European nurse who was working in the islands and as she watched this form of dancing with all its sexual overtones, a spirit of lust entered her. She told those of us who were seeking to help her that, if her husband knew about this deliverance he would be extremely upset. For some weeks we tried to see her delivered but every time we thought she was delivered, this demon voice would speak out of her in a demonic tongue. Finally, in desperation, we called in the husband and found of course that the demon had been lying. We had been listening to a lying voice instead of listening to the Holy Spirit because the husband was greatly distressed when he saw the demon activity in his wife. He was immediately sympathetic, and as we prayed a tremendous deliverance took place. The demon language which was coming out of the woman's mouth included certain words from the Cook Islands and, from this, the husband was able to tell us of that particular dance. As the woman renounced the spirit that had entered her at that dance it left with a tremendous noise, and she was finally set free. That spirit of lust had entered through her eyes as she was watching the dance.

It thus behoves us to be very careful of what we watch and listen to at all times.

SPIRITUAL FORCES WITH WHICH WE MUST NOT HAVE CONTACT:

1. FORBIDDEN SPIRITUAL CONTACTS
   Deut. 18:9-14

> "When you come into the land which the Lord your God is giving you, you shall not learn to follow the abominations of those nations.
> "There shall not be found among you anyone who makes his son or his daughter pass through the fire, or one who practices witchcraft, or a soothsayer, or one who interprets omens, or a sorcerer,
> "or one who conjures spells, or a medium, or a spiritist, or one who calls up the dead.
> "For all who do these things are an abomination to the Lord, and because of these abominations the Lord your God drives them out from before you.
> "You shall be blameless before the Lord your God.
> "For these nations which you will dispossess listened to

soothsayers and diviners; but as for you, the Lord your God has not appointed such for you."

It is clear from this that we must not allow our children to take part in demonic ceremonies such as walking through the fires. In Fiji and other countries it is common for firewalking to take place whereby the participants prepare themselves for up to a week beforehand, allowing demon forces to take over their body, particularly hypnotism. Hypnotism is one of the greatest forms of demonic activity, and if we have ever gone through such forms of healing, then it must be totally renounced.

After a week or so of such activity, the participants are able to walk on red hot stones without it affecting their body. This form of satanic miracle draws many thousands to watch but they are in danger of the demons entering them as they watch this activity. These spiritual ceremonies of course are not Christian but are totally demonic in origin having their beginnings in Hinduism. These types of miracles were of course known in heathen lands surrounding Israel in Old Testament times and God forbade His people to enter into those contacts.

During the course of these activities I saw many parents encouraging their children to receive the demons which are present in those walking through the fire. These demons manifest more boldly as the children grow older. Recently in India we witnessed people walking with arrows through their cheeks and pieces of iron through their throat. These miracles were accomplished under demonic powers. The pieces of iron and darts had been thrust through their cheeks and throat that morning without apparent ill effects. Later in the week they would be withdrawn from the bodies of those people.

CURSES FROM GOD

It is also clear from scripture that, those who practise witchcraft or are soothsayers, or interpret omens, or sorcerers, or conjure up spells, are under a curse from God. Similarly, spiritists or those who call the dead, are doing things which are an abomination to God. We, of course, know that we cannot have communication with the dead; it is purely a demon to whom we are talking. Many people are puzzled by spiritism, and the fact that these spirits seem to know all about the dead persons. We must recognize that these demonic forces can follow those persons who are not fully committed to Jesus Christ during their lives, with the result that they can take note of our address, the clothes we wear, and other personal details. If we go to a spiritist or medium, that medium will call up that spirit which claims it is the dead person and the demon will speak about the dead person with personal and intimate knowledge because it has followed that dead person during their lifetime.

2. CONTACTING THE DEAD

Recently there have been some teachings relating to healing whereby the minister has purported to deal with the spirits of dead persons still seeking a home. This scripture is perfectly clear:

> "*And as it is appointed for men to die once, but after this the judgment.*" (Heb.9:27)

In this particular ministry, there have been real results of healing. There has been confusion over the spirits with whom the minister is dealing. The spirits are not those of the dead but are familiar spirits, namely family spirits that have come down through the generations.

3. FORTUNE-TELLING

We must remember that the spirit of divination operates by revelation and predicting the future. Reading of horoscopes and the like are forbidden by scripture. Similarly, such things as extra-sensory perception and the like are a form of divination. All of this is operating through another spirit.

Let us remember the scripture:

> "*Stand now with your enchantments and the multitude of your sorceries, in which you have laboured from your youth — perhaps you will be able to profit, perhaps you will prevail.*
>
> *You are wearied in the multitude of your counsels; let now the astrologers, the star-gazers, and the monthly*

prognosticators stand up and save you from these things that shall come upon you."(Isaiah 47:12,13)

4. WITCHCRAFT

Similarly, in the case of witchcraft, we see spells and curses as well as hypnotic spirits operating. There are many witches' covens set up around the world and they seek to place curses on Christians and others. Even in Auckland, New Zealand, we have found cases of Christians becoming sick as spells have been placed upon them. When we have realized the source of the problem, we have been able to bind those spirits and the Christians have been delivered.

Thus, the scriptures are very clear that we are to keep away from witchcraft, sorcery and spiritism, as well as fortune-telling and horoscopes. The use of charms is also forbidden. There are many such counterfeits operating in the world today, intended to mislead the Christian. We see and read of people who can bend spoons by their thought life, and magicians in India who have tremendous followings and who are capable of great miracles. A friend of mine watched one such miracle worker on one occasion and is certain that he saw him turn sand into a coin right in front of his eyes.

5. SORCERY

The spirit of sorcery operates through charms as well as music and dancing and drugs. It is one of the great curses referred to in the Bible.

Let us look at some of the scriptures:

"But there was a certain man called Simon, who previously practiced sorcery in the city and astonished the people of Samaria, claiming that he was someone great,

to whom they all gave heed, from the least to the greatest, saying, 'This man is the great power of God.'

And they heeded him because he had astonished them with his sorceries for a long time." (Acts 8:9-11)

We notice that Simon the sorcerer had bewitched them with sorceries, and when he saw the Holy Spirit power, he sought to buy it. Peter's response is set out in Verse 23:

"For I see that you are poisoned by bitterness and bound by iniquity." (Acts 8:23)

PAUL AND ELYMAS

Again, we read of Elymas, the sorcerer in Acts 13:

"Now when they had gone through the island to Paphos, they found a certain sorcerer, a false prophet, a Jew whose name was Bar-Jesus,

who was with the proconsul, Sergius Paulus, an intelligent man. This man called for Barnabas and Saul and sought to hear the word of God.

But Elymas the sorcerer (for so his name is translated) withstood them, seeking to turn the proconsul away from the faith.

Then Saul, who also is called Paul, filled with the Holy Spirit, looked intently at him

and said, 'O full of all deceit and all

fraud, you son of the devil, you enemy of all righteousness, will you not cease from perverting the straight ways of the Lord?

"And now, indeed, the hand of the Lord is upon you, and you shall be blind, not seeing the sun for a time." And immediately a dark mist fell on him, and he went around seeking someone to lead him by the hand.

Then the proconsul believed, when he saw what had been done, being astonished at the teaching of the Lord." (Acts 13:6-12)

GALATIANS

Paul had to rebuke the Galatians as they went into error, and we find this in Galatians 3:

"O foolish Galatians! Who has bewitched you that you should not obey the truth, before whose eyes Jesus Christ was clearly portrayed among you as crucified?" (Galatians 3:1)

"But now after you have known God, or rather are known by God, how is it that you turn again to the weak and beggarly elements, to which you desire again to be in bondage?

You observe days and months and seasons and years.

I am afraid for you, least I have laboured for you in vain." (Galatians 4:9-11)

The last words with regard to sorcery are set out in Revelation:

"But the rest of mankind, who were not killed by these plagues, did not repent of the works of their hands, that they

should not worship demons, and idols of gold, silver, brass, stone, and wood, which can neither see nor hear nor walk; and they did not repent of their murders or their sorceries or their sexual immorality or their thefts." (Rev.9:20,21)

"*But the cowardly, unbelieving, abominable, murderers, sexually immoral, sorcerers, idolators, and all liars shall have their part in the lake which burns with fire and brimstone, which is the second death.*" (Rev.21:8)

."*And the light of a lamp shall not shine in you anymore. And the voice of bridegroom and bride shall not be heard in you anymore. For your merchants were the great men of the earth, for by your sorcery all the nations were deceived.*" (Rev.18:23)

It is imperative that we renounce all of these forbidden contacts and sever all contact with them: In Ephesus the converts burnt their books on magic.

"*This became known both to all Jews and Greeks dwelling in Ephesus; and fear fell on them all, and the name of the Lord Jesus was magnified.*

And many who had believed came, confessing and telling their deeds.

Also, many of those who had practiced magic brought their books together and burned them in the sight of all. And they counted up the value of them, and it totalled fifty thousand pieces of silver." (Acts 19:17-19)

6. CHARMS AND FETISHES IN OUR HOMES

It is especially important to remove from our home lucky charms, fetishes, Buddhas carvings and anything which relates to witchcraft. Many people have been released from depression and other spiritual attacks by doing so. The scripture is very clear in this regard:

> "You shall burn the carved images of their gods with fire; you shall not covet the silver or gold that is on them, nor take it for yourselves, lest you be snared by it; for it is an abomination to the Lord your God.
> Nor shall you bring an abomination into your house, lest you be doomed to destruction like it; but you shall utterly detest it and utterly abhor it, for it is an accursed thing."
> (Deut. 7:25,26)

We find in the New Testament that this is exactly what happened in the Book of Acts: In the scripture quoted above (Acts 19:17-19).

At the end of this book, I have attached a list of modern forms of sorcery and witchcraft. You should read them through and mark those with which you have ever been involved, and renounce them specifically.

7. YOGA

Some people cannot understand the problem that lies behind martial arts and practices such as acupuncture and yoga. We must always look at the PHILOSOPHY which is behind a particular practice. For example, in the case of yoga, we may well do the exercises thinking there is no problem associated with them, but many of the exercises are positions of worship to demon gods. Thus, behind the practice of yoga is the occultic element of worship, and as we practice yoga we invite these spirits to attach themselves to us.

8. ACUPUNCTURE

Similarly, in the case of acupuncture, we find it goes back to Emperor Huang Ti who concluded, through a study of the stars, that harmony and balance exist in the universe. There is a definite input from astrology in this practice. There is a reference to an energy or life force called Ch'i which is supposed to go into the body at birth and out again at death. This flows through the body in two systems, namely Yang — which is the male principle, and represents the sun — and the female principle, Yin, which represents the moon.

Yang and Yin are supposed to flow through the body by a system of canals called the meridians which, in turn, go under the skin and around the body with fourteen main ones linked by 15 luo canals and 47 subsidiary meridians, passing close to the skin at 365 points.

It is not hard to see that just below this practice there is a philosophy involving the sun, the moon, the days of the year.

I firmly believe there are psychic powers behind the practice of acupuncture and even its most innocent form can bring spiritual oppression. There can be a physical healing which takes place, as frequently happens when we use occultic practices in medicine, and with that comes a spiritual oppression.

9. MARTIAL ARTS

Again, in such practices, as karate, kung-fu, and judo, I have found that those involved in these receive spirits of violence and anger which manifest in an extreme fashion when we pray for deliverance.

Always look at the philosophy behind the practice, not the practice only, and if you make a full study of that philosophy you will soon determine whether it is based upon God's Word or whether it is a philosophy from the pit of hell.

"And no wonder! For Satan himself transforms himself into an angel of light." (2 Cor. 11:14)

10. IRIDOLOGY

Another practice which is becoming increasingly common is the practice of iridology, or iris diagnosis. Like acupuncture, this goes back to Chinese forms of healing originating with astrology. In the case of iris diagnosis, the Chinese, some three thousand years ago divided the eye into five concentric zones. In order to make a diagnosis, alterations in these zones were checked out. Later on, there was a division into twelve fields corresponding to the astrological signs of the zodiac, Aries, Taurus, Gemini, Cancer, Leo, Virgo, Libra, Scorpio, Saggitarius, Capricorn, Aquarius, Pisces. It is perfectly clear that this practice is based upon the occult and should be totally avoided by Christians. Although healing may take place, as I have said earlier, this can well be followed by spiritual oppression, which is even worse than the physical condition apparently healed.

Thirteen

Occurences During Deliverance

We find that often there are manifestations which occur during the course of deliverance. Sometimes there is no manifestation whatsoever because the spirit goes quietly, and whichever way it occurs we are to have faith to believe it is taking place. We must not be disappointed if there is no physical sign of deliverance because quite frequently spirits do leave without any sound. However, we must always have a witness in our spirit that they have in fact left, otherwise we can be deceived.

On other occasions, however, there are clear manifestations as they go. This is confirmed in the Book of Acts:

"*For unclean spirits, crying with a loud voice, came out of many who were possessed; and many who were paralyzed and lame were healed.*" (Acts 8:7)

I have seen all the following forms of manifestations occur:

Hissing, coughing, screaming, spitting, belching, roaring, vomiting, sobbing, trembling, violent shaking, vile smells.

BARKING

Sometimes men and women get on their hands and knees and bark like dogs. In one such incident in our home the housekeeper came running through the house trying to find the dog which she thought was in the house. Barking can be as realistic as this. Sometimes people often shake their heads violently as though to say 'no'. On another occasion I saw a boy lie on the church floor barking like a dog at the moon. As the spirit left him and he was set totally free he changed his personality back to the real person whom God had created. I have seen a man rushing forward on his hands and knees and baring his teeth as he made towards the altar rail in our church during a deliverance session. The Vicar told me that if the altar rail had not been strongly constructed he wondered what would have happened. I have simply withstood such cases in the name of Jesus and the person stopped short of the rail. The spirit of a lion has come out on occasions.

SLITHERING

I have also seen many cases where the person has begun to slither like a snake along the floor. Often the head or body has moved at such a speed from side to side that it is impossible for the human eye to follow. In the Suva Cathedral several years ago when I took authority in the name of Jesus over the spirit of Dirga, many Hindus fell on the floor and then slithered like snakes over and under the pews making tremendous roaring and belching noises as they slithered.

The demonic power which takes people over is sometimes manifested by the people laying on their back and slithering backwards; at the same time their whole body moves violently from side to side at great speed.

FEIGNING DEATH

On other occasions a person may lay still as though dead. This is similar to the case referred to in scripture:

"Then the Spirit cried out, convulsed him greatly, and came out of him. And he became as one dead, so that many said, "He is dead".

But Jesus took him by the hand and lifted him up, and he arose." (Mark 9:26,27)

In those cases I have also taken the hand of the person and asked them to come up in the name of Jesus at the same time rebuking the spirit of death which seems to come over them.

DEMONS IN THE EYES

On occasions we can look into the eyes of the person who is being delivered and we can see the little "piggy eyes" of the demon. When the demon realises you are looking at him, the person's eyes will shut very tightly to prevent you from seeing the demon. In those cases I often open the eyelids and look into the eyes of the person to command the demon to come out.

When we are ministering against spirits which have been in animals and are now in people, we may find that they have on occasions taken the person's own name so that if you are ministering to a person called John you will also find a false John there. He will take over the true John's personality and on these occasions also his voice so that you must check from time to time to ensure that you are speaking to the correct John. As repentance and true deliverance take place, the false person leaves.

MISCELLANEOUS MANIFESTATIONS

We must remember that Satan often takes the form of a serpent and it is not uncommon to hear a hissing sound come out of the person's mouth as the demon begins to leave. On one occasion I heard a demon hissing from a person's fingers.

Quite frequently I have found that the demons are in the saliva and the Holy Spirit encourages me to have people spit them out.

In another manifestation the tongue often goes in and out like a snake's tongue. Sometimes the tongue protrudes from the mouth.

In the case of demons of sexual uncleanliness it is quite common for white foam to come out of the person's mouth. I have seen it come out by the bucketfull. These are not demons but are the nests in which the demons have lived.

Demons of fear frequently sob or whisper and lying and hatred demons often make a loud noise like a roar. The demon of smoking seems to come out with a cough or a gasp. Often the demon uses the person's voice and you can quite clearly hear that the voice has changed. It will frequently become more highly pitched but is distinctly different.

Demons will sometimes give their names and when commanded so to do, I have heard them speak out the names of hatred, bitterness, envy, jealousy, fear, suicide, adultery, witchcraft, mockery, blasphemy, perversity, schizophrenia and death.

Violence can be manifested by the person showing supernatural strength. Fingers sometimes become twisted and people will complain of tingling in them. Masturbation is sometimes manifested by the movement of the fingers. Sometimes blood comes out of the mouth as demons tear the flesh as they leave.

Many times when demons are leaving there is a strong sulphur-like smell which is most unpleasant. This is the opposite of the beautiful fragrance of the Holy Spirit which is often manifested when we are praising God.

In my experience I do not find that demons of oppression make any specific sound when leaving but as a rule the person feels lighter and they will often say,

"I feel lighter, something has gone."

NAMES OF DEMONS

Sometimes during a lengthy deliverance the Holy Spirit gives us the names of the demons in sequence. Frequently they are in clusters and the same demon may appear in different clusters of demons. For example under the heading of bitterness we may find hatred, unforgiveness, anger, weakness, false name, violence. Again, under another cluster headed up by strife we may also find bitterness, unforgiveness, hatred and resentment.

MOCKERY

Sometimes the demons will openly mock us and we can see the person's face twisted as the spirit of mockery comes upon them. Here again we can take authority over the spirit but we must have the co-operation of the person concerned by them showing true repentance. When I speak of co-operation I am referring to those situations where the person has their natural senses and abilities, not those, for example, where there has been brain damage or some other condition which will require the sovereign act of the Holy Spirit for both deliverance and healing as we act in faith. In such instances we can command the spirits to leave and then pray for the person's total healing and deliverance.

YAWNING

Another frequent manifestation of demons leaving is yawning. Sometimes these particular demons cause people to go to sleep during meetings, particularly when the gospel is being preached. Sometimes yawning is also accompanied by sighing as demons leave a person.

PRIDE

The spirit of pride can manifest itself by the person standing or sitting in a very erect position and folding their arms across the chest. This is often manifested by the spirit calling itself self-importance.

FEAR AND TENSION

Spirits of fear and tension can cause pain in the back of our head or in our neck.

FALSE SLAYING IN THE SPIRIT

Sometimes demons will manifest by making the person extremely heavy and cause them to fall on the floor. This can easily be mistaken for true slaying in the Spirit or resting in the Spirit as it is sometimes called. If we are in any doubt we should ask the person to stand up and usually at this point it can be clearly discerned whether the person has really been slain in the Spirit or whether they are being oppressed by a demon when they will feel a tremendous heaviness in their body. This is opposite to the slaying in the Spirit, where there is usually a lightness as people float down like a feather.

Remember the demons are extremely cunning and will always seek to hide from you. They will use every method open to them to hide, including causing people to fall to the ground.

FOURTEEN

Domination and Matriarchal Spirits

This can be a form of witchcraft . . . it does not matter whether we are an Anglican witch, a Pentecostal witch, a Presbyterian witch, or whatever. If we, as adults, seek to control our children in an unscriptural manner and dominate them, then we are subject to the spirit of witchcraft operating through us. I believe that this is important for all of us to be careful about, particularly those of us who are in some form of authority, whether we be employer, pastors, parent. If we have a strong or dominating spirit then it can bind those under us, and as we go into error, so we will lead those who are subject to our authority. The opposite of this is put in a beautiful way in scripture:

"The elders who are among you I exhort, I who am a fellow elder and a witness of the sufferings of Christ, and also a partaker of the glory that will be revealed:

Shepherd the flock of God which is among you, serving as overseers, not by constraint but willingly, not for dishonest gain but eagerly;

nor as being lords over those entrusted to you, but being examples to the flock;

and when the Chief Shepherd appears, you will receive the crown of glory that does not fade away.

Likewise you younger people, submit yourselves to your elders. Yes, all of you be submissive to one another, and be clothed with humility, for

"God resists the proud,
But gives grace to the humble."

Therefore humble yourselves under the mighty hand of God, that he may exalt you in due time." (1 Peter 5:1-6)

Remember that Jesus, in one of His last actions on this earth, washed the feet of His disciples. We must always keep a humble spirit, and in this way prevent the spirit of deception from entering us.

WRONG EXAMPLE

On many occasions I have seen disaster strike churches where the pastor has taken absolute authority over his flock, believing that he is hearing from God. When members of his flock have spoken to him concerning certain reservations, they have been told they are in rebellion. Invariably, the pastor of that church has himself fallen from grace as he has entered into some deception or error and considerable division has occurred within that church.

MATRIARCHAL SPIRITS

I have freqently found in meetings that, when I have spoken about the spirit of domination and asked those who believe that they have been dominated by their mother to raise their hand, up to seventy five per cent of those present in the meeting have done so. This form of domination can work in many ways. It is especially subtle in parent-in-law relationships. It is a leading cause of break-up of marriages, as well as causing many women to feel rejected and unable to cope with problems within their marriage. Similarly, men who have been subject to domination often have homosexual tendencies or are weak and unable to face up to their responsibilities in marriage. It is totally unscriptural for parents to dominate their children in such a way that, as they grow older, there is still a hold over those children.

It is very clear from scripture that we must obey those who rule over us and be submissive, for they watch over our souls as those who must give account, (Heb.13:17). Nevertheless those in authority must be very careful that they, too, are in submission to the part of the body of Christ to whom they minister, in accordance with 1 Peter 5:5, quoted above, otherwise there is a great danger of deception entering.

As an evangelist, I always submit to the authority of those who call me to a particular situation. I find great blessing as I kneel down and ask those who have called me, whether they be pastors, layman, or both, to pray over me for God's blessing. As I humble myself in these circumstances, I find that the anointing of God invariably falls and healings and deliverances follow.

PASTOR IN BONDAGE

On another occasion, a pastor came to me and stated that he had had forty years' experience in the ministry but that he had now lost all power in his ministry. He was a man of 63 years of age and told me that he had spent 25 years in the Salvation Army, then 15 years in a Pentecostal church which did not believe that Christians could have demons. The Holy Spirit indicated to me that I should ask him about his mother, and I did so. The response was immediate. A snarling voice came out of the man stating that he hated his mother. I asked the age of the man's mother and he stated that she was 93 years old and he stated further that she had always dominated him.

I took him up to my hotel room and began to pray. After a short time he got down on his hands and knees and then the dominating spirit which had come from his mother began to manifest itself on him. He began to shake like a dog coming out of the water. We all know how a dog shakes the water off itself when it comes out of the tide, and in the same way this man had a violent shaking on the back of his neck where the demon was attached.

It had spoken to his mind over many years and was a

demon of domination from his mother. As I counselled him to forgive his mother, to honour her and to pray afresh for her, the spirit came loose. He finally vomited across the floor as the spirit came out of him, and finally stood up completely free.

Subsequently that church changed its teaching which said that a Christian could not have a demon.

DOMINANT WIFE

When a marriage becomes unbalanced, for example when the wife becomes the dominating force, then various unscriptural results follow. We have already remarked on how the spirit of homosexuality can enter boys who are brought up in this type of home. God's order is clearly set out:

> *"But I want you to know that the head of every man is Christ, the head of woman is man, and the head of Christ is God."* (1 Cor. 11:3)

When this scriptural order is departed from then Satan has a legal right to enter and cause havoc in that situation.

I have come across many cases where the spirit of domination is clearly manifested as the child of the spirit of Jezebel, about which we spoke in Chapter 4. This takes the form of a controlling spirit over a pastor through his wife and it can affect the whole church.

It has been suggested that some women take a subtle form of control over their husbands through the use of their own body. As the marriage progresses they tend to exercise control over their husband's thought life and actions through a dominating spirit. This is of course disastrous, particularly in the case of churches where the spirit of Jezebel can literally destroy the work of God by causing divisions and spiritual death. One outworking of this situation can often be promiscuous children of believing parents, including pastors.

This form of domination has been manifested in these latter days in some forms of unscriptural teaching which have required members of the body of Christ to submit themselves to others in such a way that their every action had to be approved by another person. Where practised this has invariably led to dissension and division because it is clearly not from God. Those who complain, or those who take a stand against such forms of domination have been told that they are rebellious and out of order.

Praise God, the body of Christ as a whole has discerned this error and we find this type of doctrine diminishing. However, it will occur again if we do not keep a balance in the Word of God at all times.

MARRIAGE BREAKDOWN

I have found from long experience that a prime cause of tension in marriage is a spirit of witchcraft. This can come down through the parents of either the husband or wife, or both. Until it is dealt with, the problem will remain.

FIFTEEN

Who should pray for Deliverance

The word says:

> "And these signs will follow those who believe: In my name they will cast out demons; they will speak with new tongues;" (Mark 16:17)

This scripture makes it perfectly clear that all believers should have a "signs following" ministry and all believers are capable of casting out demons. Although some people may have a greater ability in this area than others, it behoves all Christians to know their authority in Jesus Christ to deal with demonic forces. It has been my great pleasure to minister with an increasing number of ordinary men and women who are committed to Jesus Christ and to see how they have learnt to operate effectively in the ministry of deliverance. With the breakdown in society and the greater manifestation of demon powers almost daily, it is necessary for us to understand our authority in Jesus Christ. However, in order to do so, we must be born again of the Spirit of God and be filled with the Holy Spirit.

REQUIREMENTS FOR PERSON MINISTERING DELIVERANCE:

Unless we have had a personal encounter with the Lord Jesus Christ and have allowed Him to be not only Saviour of our life but also Our Lord, as well as Baptizer in the Holy Spirit, then we will lack the authority which is required to minister deliverance.

JESUS AS LORD

Among other things, the scriptures clearly show us that Jesus is the Saviour and should also be Lord of our life. We need to surrender our thought life, our emotional life, and every part of our being to His Lordship, so that we can be completely filled with the Holy Spirit.

JESUS AS BAPTIZER IN HOLY SPIRIT

In each of the Gospels, Jesus is described as the Baptizer in the Holy Spirit and we remember that in Luke 24:49, He told His disciples to wait in Jerusalem until they received the promise of the Father.

Jesus stated these words after He had already breathed on His disciples and they had received the Holy Spirit on the Sunday night of His resurrection:

> "And when he had said this, he breathed on them, and said to them, "Receive the Holy Spirit." (John 20:22)

This command was repeated in Acts 1:4 & 8, and as the disciples waited in the upper room, we find in Acts 2:1-4 that the Holy Spirit fell upon them. Following this, Peter preached his first sermon under the anointing of the Holy Spirit, and was able to explain what had happened, namely that they were not drunk as was supposed but that the Holy Spirit had fallen upon them in accordance with the prophecy spoken by the prophet Joel:

> *"And it shall come to pass afterwards that I will pour out my Spirit on all flesh; your sons and your daughters shall prophesy, your old men shall dream dreams, your young men shall see visions;*
>
> *And also on my menservants and on my maidservants I will pour out my Spirit in those days."* (Joel 2:28,29)
>
> *"I will show wonders in heaven above and signs in the earth beneath: Blood and fire and vapor of smoke.*
>
> *The sun shall be turned into darkness, and the moon into blood, before the coming of the great and notable day of the Lord."* (Acts 2:19,20)

PROMISE OF THE FATHER

Finally, Peter was able to point out that Jesus was now exalted at the right hand of God and had received from the Father the promise of the Holy Spirit which He had poured out and which they could now see and hear.

> *"Therefore being exalted to the right hand of God, and*

> *having received from the Father the promise of the Holy Spirit, He poured out this which you now see and hear."* (Acts 2:33)

GIFTS OF THE HOLY SPIRIT

As we move on in the power of the Holy Spirit, we find that there are gifts of the Holy Spirit, as set out in 1 Corinthians 12, including the gift of discernment of spirits. The other gifts of the word of knowledge, the gift of faith, and the word of wisdom are also important to the deliverance ministry.

In my book, "Receiving the Gifts of the Holy Spirit", I describe how I came into the gift of discernment of spirits. I find this, like the other gifts of the word of knowledge and word of wisdom, can be impressions, or thoughts upon my mind, or the audible voice of the Holy Spirit as well as a vision, with the result that as I minister deliverance, the Holy Spirit will show me the parts of the body to which the demons are attached, or names of the demons, or both, and how to pray.

THE AUTHORITY OF THE MINISTER:

We must understand the authority which is given to us in the name of Jesus:

> *"Then Jesus came and spoke to them, saying, 'All authority has been given to me in heaven and on earth.'"* (Matt. 28:18)

Just as Jesus said that all authority was given to Him in heaven and earth, so must we accept that He has given us the authority to deal with demon powers.

CENTURION

The centurion was a man who understood what it was like to be under authority. In Matthew's gospel we read of the centurion coming to Jesus and asking Him to heal his servant. When Jesus offered to come and heal him, the centurion said:

". . . Lord, I am not worthy that you should come under my roof. But only speak a word, and my servant will be healed.

"For I also am a man under authority, having soldiers under me. And I say to this one, 'Go,' and he goes; and to another, 'Come,' and he comes; and to my servant, 'Do this,' and he does it."

When Jesus heard it, he marveled, and said to those who followed, "Assuredly, I say to you, I have not found such great faith, not even in Israel!" (Matt.8:8-10)

"And Jesus said to the centurion, "Go your way; and as you have believed, so let it be done for you." And his servant was healed that same hour." (Matt.8:13)

The centurion understood that not only was he a man under authority, but that Jesus Christ was under the authority of God the Father. It is when we come to understand the authority which Jesus has given us, and the authority that is in his name, then because we are people under authority, we will see real manifestations of deliverance.

MAN UNDER AUTHORITY

Whenever I am praying for a person, I am always looking to Jesus and thinking of the authority which He gives me from God. As I look up at the line of authority, the demon powers understand that I am doing so and they begin to tremble. I will often say to a demon that I am under the authority of my Lord and Master, Jesus Christ, who has trodden down the authority of his lord and master, Satan. When the demon realizes that I mean this, it will begin to tremble and flee. I believe this is one of the great KEYS to exercising the deliverance ministry, that is, knowing our authority in Jesus Christ.

Remember that the demons will be watching our every move as we pray, and if we doubt our authority, that doubt shows up immediately and the demon will gain the upper hand. This is why we must have complete belief in the authenticity of the Word of God.

ABSOLUTE BELIEF IN THE WORD OF GOD

We must believe the Word of God in our heart, and not just in our mind.

The person carrying out the deliverance must have a total faith and belief that the Word of God is absolutely true in every respect. If he has any doubts concerning the Word of God, the demons will know it and will not move.

Demons immediately know whether we really believe what we are saying and whether we are really born again in our spirit and believe the Word of God in our heart.

At a seminar in New Zealand consisting of a large number of men who claimed to be born again, Spirit-filled Christians, one of them manifested a demon of lust. As I prayed against this demon, I recited certain scriptures and the demon began to manifest in violent reaction. I then called upon the other thirty men present and suggested that we recite together the Word of God. This was to show them the power of the Word of God against demon power. As we recited various scriptures, such as John 3:16 . . .

"For God so loved the world that he gave his only begotton Son, that whoever believes in him should not perish but have everlasting life."

The demon manifested more and more violently until it finally left the man, who was set free.

INTELLECTUAL CHRISTIANITY

In giving his testimony the following morning, the man who had been set free made the following startling statement: He said that, as we were praying for him, the demon voice spoke to him and said that he would not have had to go if only 15 of the men had been there.

This particular 15, he said, only believed the Word of God in their mind and not in their heart. The other 15, however, did believe the Word of God in their heart and consequently he had to go because of them.

This is clear evidence that we must not be intellectual Christians but Christians who are born again of the Spirit of God, totally committed to the Lordship of Jesus Christ, if we are to have an effective ministry against demon power.

BLOOD SCRIPTURES

We need to have a clear understanding and belief in the Blood Scriptures which I have set out in Appendix 2. We can never over estimate the power that is in the blood of Jesus. The demons know this power and they know whether we really believe in that power.

The tremendous power that is in the blood of Jesus must be known to every Christian and believed by him if he is going to be an effective minister.

The person ministering must clearly understand how the precious blood of Jesus purchased us from the hand of the devil and how through that same blood, all our sins have been forgiven. Many times I have heard the demons scream as I have recited the words from Revelation . . .

> *"And they overcame him by the blood of the Lamb and by the word of their testimony."* (Rev.12:11)

I usually have people say that the word of their testimony is that Jesus is their Lord.

WE MUST AVOID PRIDE

As we are ministering, the demons will know whether we have pride and will begin to build upon it. They can do this by making us believe that we are really accomplishing something when in fact we are not getting the person delivered at all. We must at all times keep ourselves humble before God and recall what Jesus said about His disciples. When the seventy returned with joy saying, "Lord, even the demons are subject to us in your name", His response is set out in Luke 10:

> "*And he said to them, 'I saw Satan fall like lightning from heaven.*
> "*Behold, I give you the authority to trample on serpents and scorpions, and over all the power of the enemy, and nothing shall by any means hurt you.*
> "*Nevertheless do not rejoice in this, that the spirits are subject to you, but rejoice rather because your names are written in heaven.*" (Luke 10:18-20)

FRUIT OF THE HOLY SPIRIT

Remember, too, that we are not judged by the gifts of the Spirit in our lives but by the fruit of the Holy Spirit. Many will say that they have cast out demons and prophesied in the name of Jesus, but will not enter the kingdom of God:

> "Not everyone who says to me, 'Lord, Lord,' shall enter the kingdom of heaven, but he who does the will of my Father in heaven.
>
> "Many will say to me in that day, 'Lord, Lord, have we not prophesied in your name, cast out demons in your name, and done many wonders in your name?'
>
> "And then I will declare to them, 'I never knew you; depart from me, you who practice lawlessness!'"
> (Matt.7:21-23)

We must always ensure that the fruit of the Holy Spirit is operating in our lives:

> "But the fruit of the Spirit is love, joy, peace, long-suffering, kindness, goodness, faithfulness,
>
> gentleness, self-control. Against such there is no law."
> (Gal.5:22,23)

Remember that demons can read our mind. I know that this horrifies many Christians but I have found it to be true during the time that I have ministered. Sometimes they have told me that I am tired or that I have something else to do, or I have another appointment ... all of which is perfectly true. Accordingly, we must always keep our mind totally centred upon Jesus as Saviour and be totally surrendered to Him, if we are going to operate in this ministry, in the power which Jesus would have us do.

SIXTEEN

How to Receive your Deliverance

1. FAITH

It is important that the person to be delivered is encouraged to exercise faith in Jesus Christ. Accordingly, they must receive Jesus Christ as their personal Saviour and if possible be baptized with the Holy Spirit before deliverance takes place. Again, water baptism is imperative if they have never experienced it. On the other hand if they are not open to the baptism of the Holy Spirit at that stage, they should be counselled concerning this experience. We must exercise the love and wisdom that God gives us in these matters.

Accordingly, they should be encouraged to have an expectant faith in Jesus Christ for their deliverance. As they are encouraged to think of Jesus Christ seated at the right hand of God as their Mediator and Intercessor before God and their great High Priest, then the Holy Spirit can move freely against the conditions binding them.

2. REPENTANCE

I believe that repentance is the key to the door in every circumstance. It is the key to the door of salvation, healing, baptism in the Spirit, and deliverance.

We remember that John the Baptist preached a baptism of repentance for the remission of sin. Among the first words which Jesus preached were:

> *"The time is fulfilled, and the kingdom of God is at hand. Repent, and believe in the gospel."* (Mark 1:15)

Yes, repentance is the key that opens all doors, and before we can expect a lasting deliverance, true repentance must take place. Remorse means being sorry for our sins, whereas repentance means turning ABSO-LUTELY from our sins. There is a world of difference. Judas showed remorse, but not repentance. Thus in Matthew we read:

> *"Then Judas, his betrayer, seeing that he had been condemned, was remorseful and brought back the thirty pieces of silver to the chief priests and elders."* (Matt. 27:3)

Judas did not show repentance, he only showed remorse. Repentance means an absolute turning around from everything that is dark in our lives to the light of Jesus Christ. Jesus expressed it beautifully when He spoke to Paul on the Damascus Road:

> *"I will deliver you from the Jewish people, as well as from the Gentiles, to whom I now send you,*

"to open their eyes and to turn them from darkness to light, and from the power of Satan to God, that they may receive forgiveness of sins and an inheritance among those who are sanctified by faith in me." (Acts 26:17,18)

A DECISION

Thus true repentance is having our spiritual eyes opened and turning from darkness to light, and from the power of Satan to God. But this is a DECISION on our part, an act of our will, and herein lies the key to our salvation and deliverance.

"Repent" was the word spoken by Jesus at the beginning of his earthly ministry and we find that when He appeared to John on the isle of Patmos, towards the end of John's life and spoke of the seven churches, in the case of five of them, he stated the need for them to repent. Thus, repentance is at the beginning and at the end of the New Testament and the key to our understanding of the New Testament, rests upon repentance.

The disciples went out and preached that people should repent, and as a result they cast out many demons and anointed with oil many who were sick, and healed them:

"So they went out and preached that people should repent.

And they cast out many demons, and anointed with oil many who were sick, and healed them." (Mark 6:12,13)

PRODIGAL SON

Again, we remember the parable of the prodigal son who left home. When he was in the midst of all his squalor feeding the pigs and would gladly have eaten the same food as the pigs, he came to his senses and made a DECISION TO GO BACK TO HIS FATHER. He said:

> "I will arise and go to my father, and will say to him, 'Father, I have sinned against heaven and before you,
>
> "and I am no longer worthy to be called your son. Make me like one of your hired servants.'
>
> "And he arose and came to his father. But when he was still a great way off, his father saw him and had compassion, and ran and fell on his neck and kissed him."
> (Luke 15:18-20)

Here we see him making a decision and carrying it out. This is true repentance . . . an act of our own will.

NEED FOR TRUE REPENTANCE

I am convinced, from many years of experience in the deliverance ministry, that unless there is true repentance, there will be no lasting deliverance. There must be an ABSOLUTE turning from sin and a DECISION of our will to stay away from sin. As we are told in Romans Chapter 6, our old man was crucified with Jesus so that the body of sin might be done away with and we should no longer be slaves of sin.

> "Likewise you also, reckon yourselves to be dead

indeed to sin, but alive to God in Christ Jesus our Lord.
"Therefore do not let sin reign in your mortal body,
that you should obey it in its lusts.
"And do not present your members as instruments of
unrighteousness to sin, but present yourselves to God as
being alive from the dead, and your members as instru-
ments of righteousness to God.
"For sin shall not have dominion over you, for you are
not under the law but under grace." (Romans 6:11-14)

Here sin is spoken of as something we can obey or turn from. I believe from my personal experience that behind every sin there is a spirit from Satan, and if we embark upon the path of sin, then the demon powers begin to descend upon us and enter into our bodies.

HOLINESS

We are called to holiness, and this is the best way both of receiving and retaining our deliverance. However, as a result of prolonged exposure to sin on our part, or that of our parents, many of us need deliverance and that is why the deliverance ministry is for the body of Christ.

Specific ways in which we can repent are as follows:—

We must humble ourselves.

As the scripture said, "Except ye be converted and become as a little child, ye shall not enter the kingdom of God."

We must become as a little child to be converted, that is we must put aside all our natural understanding and come to Jesus in true humility accepting Him as our Saviour and making Him Lord of our life.

In the same way, in order to receive Jesus as Baptizer in the Holy Spirit, we again must humble ourselves, turning from all sin and letting Him carry out this mighty ministry for us.

The whole of Jesus' ministry talked of humility. We recall that Satan fell through pride in the first place and, in my experience, there are four downward steps:—

> Pride
> Rebellion
> Deception
> Perversion of the flesh and of the spirit.

Once we allow pride to enter, then rebellion soon follows. We will not listen to anybody or be corrected by anybody. We then allow the spirit of deception in and finally we begin to allow perversion of the flesh and of the spirit. Perversion of the spirit is, of course, occultic activity and following other spirits, while perversion of the flesh can take the form of sexual immorality.

3. WE MUST CONFESS OUR SINS

Confession of sin is part of repentance and a wonderful way in which we can be delivered and healed.

"Confess your trespasses to one another, and pray for one another, that you may be healed . . ." (James 5:16)

Confession is part of healing and deliverance.

I well recall a young lady with whom we prayed during a number of years for deliverance. The demons continued to manifest and even though many came out we could not get the chief demon to go. Usually we find that there is a principal demon and many other demons are associated with him. He seems to have control over them, and until he is ousted or expelled, he continues to attract other demons back even though many may have been cast out. In this particular case, we seemed to be able to cast out many demons but still the young lady was not released. Finally, she made a confession which she had failed to do before. This happened to be a particularly filthy thing relating to witchcraft which happened before she became a Christian, and as she made the confession the demon left her. It no longer had any seat of authority in her.

I have been at many meetings where I have encouraged the sick and others to confess their sins to elders or other persons who were present. The results have often been dramatic as immediate healings have taken place. The power of God can fall in such instances and God is able to complete His perfect work of deliverance and healing.

4. HONESTY

We must be absolutely honest in our dealings with God and with one another. Our hearts must be opened to the light of God's Word. We must be honest with one another. Failure to be honest provides a further seat for Satan to sit upon with his demon power and accordingly people are not released, unless there is total honesty on their part. In cases where there has been past sin, such as adultery, I never advocate that the sinning partner goes and tells the other party to the marriage. I do not believe we are called upon to do that, but we should certainly confess that sin to another person who can be relied upon or to God Himself. The person hearing the confession must, of course, never repeat what he has heard and should forget it immediately.

We remember that there is one Mediator between God and man, and that is the man Christ Jesus, and as we confess our sins and confess His name, then He is able to intercede on our behalf before the Throne of Grace. We must be transparent if we are to receive true healing and deliverance.

5. FORGIVENESS

This is a cardinal part of repentance. Failure to forgive is one of the principal reasons why people are not released from demon power. We cannot read Matthew 18 without realizing the sovereignty of God and the need for true forgiveness. As we have remarked earlier, the only part of the Lord's Prayer which Jesus repeated was the part dealing with forgiveness. Similarly, in Matthew 18:34,35, we have the promise of God through Jesus to deliver us to the torturers (demons) if we do not, from our heart, forgive one another our trespasses.

If it was good enough for Jesus to die on the cross for each one of us and forgive us while we were still sinners, then we have no right whatsoever to have an unforgiving attitude towards others. Many times I have seen tremendous deliverance as a result of true forgiveness. I recall, on one occasion at a convention in Sydney, Australia, when a girl came forward with a crippling condition in her right arm. The Holy Spirit indicated by the word of knowledge that this girl had failed to forgive her sister. I asked the girl to do so and asked her to name her sister expressly as she forgave her. After some hesitation, the girl agreed to do so, and spoke the name of her sister, forgiving her as she did so. I asked her to say the words, "In the name of Jesus I forgive my sister Anne." She was able to say it approximately ten times and then suddenly the demon screamed out of her, "I won't, I won't, I won't forgive my sister Anne!" Once the demon had manifested it was comparatively easy to deal with it, but it was an indication of how deep demons will hide in these circumstances.

In mass meetings I often encourage people to stand and name a particular person whom they need to forgive. I usually lead them in the prayer, such as, "In the name of Jesus I forgive ..." As many names are released I have often seen dramatic healings. I recall in one Anglican church at an 8 a.m. service, I asked the congregation to do this. One or two of them walked out because they felt it was very wrong. I found that the community was a close country community with very harsh feelings working within it. However, one man who did so was released from arthritis which had bound him for over twenty years. As he forgave his brother, the spirit left him. He came along to a meeting 5 years later and testified of his absolute and complete healing. He no longer needed to take 5 pills a day.

6. CALL UPON THE NAME OF JESUS

The scriptures are specific:

> "*And it shall come to pass that whoever calls on the name of the Lord shall be saved.*" (Acts 2:21)

The word "saved" also means "delivered". If we call on Jesus to help us in such circumstances and call on Him from our heart, He always responds by giving us faith for deliverance.

7. EXERCISING OUR WILL

In all of the foregoing it can be clearly seen that there is an active ingredient of our will involved. One of the great keys to deliverance through real repentance is the fact that we use our will. Many times as we are ministering deliverance, demons try to overcome the person and fill them with fear, but I always encourage people to exercise their own will. If the demon is shouting or screaming through them, I command the demon to be quiet; I speak to the person concerned and tell him to exercise his will. I also point out that "greater is He in them than he who is in the world." (I John 4:4). We therefore need to understand clearly that this is truth and as this sinks into our spirit we realize that we really are overcomers in the name of Jesus. The person seeking deliverance must exercise his or her will in such circumstances.

In all of the foregoing instances I am speaking of the situation where the person concerned is in possession of their faculties. We, of course, read in the scriptures of the demoniac boy, but in his case the father exercised faith.

> "... *If you can believe, all things are possible to him who believes.*
> *Immediately the father of the child cried out and said with tears, 'Lord, I believe; help my unbelief!'"*
> (*Mark* 9:23,24)

There are, of course, situations where a person ministering, operating in the power of the Holy Spirit, particularly in the healing ministry, commands the demon to depart. It may be a demon of deafness or dumbness or blindness or infirmity. If the person to whom you are ministering is truly repentant then it is much easier for the demon to go, but I have seen in certain circumstances the sovereign act of God when we have taken total authority to minister in the name of Jesus and the demon has gone, even though the person themself appears to have done nothing. However, from experience, I would still believe that if that person is going to retain their deliverance there must be a true repentance with Jesus as Saviour and infilling of the Holy Spirit.

CONVERTED JEW

I recall a converted Jew coming to me on one occasion because he seemed to be so bound with anger, fear and other forces. He had received Jesus as Saviour many years earlier and had undergone the experience of the baptism of the Holy Spirit. However, he was still bound by these forces of fear and anger so badly that, in fact, his wife was thinking of leaving him. It appeared that he had undergone considerable torture and abuse in a Nazi labour camp during the war years and had never been able to overcome memories of this or to forgive his captors. I counselled him in the area of forgiveness and suggested that he went away for one week and prayed and fasted. He returned a week later, a totally changed man. He had truly sought the Lord and had researched in a bible concordance every mention of the words "forgiveness" and "repentance". He had studied every aspect from the scriptures and in the meantime had fasted. Every day for up to two hours, God brought before him as in a colour film, pictures of every person by whom he had been persecuted since the age of twelve. They showed up vividly and he sat and watched each situation as God brought it back. Jesus spoke to him concerning each situation, and as he studied the scripture carefully every day he was able to come to true repentance and forgiveness for each of those persons. By the time he saw me a week later he was totally transformed and the completion of his deliverance was only a formality. He went away rejoicing, full of the joy of the Lord and a totally new creature in Jesus Christ.

As a I prayed a simple prayer with him, the demon of hate finally left, thus he was totally released and went on his way. If anything convinced me about the ease of deliverance when there is true repentance, that particular incident certainly did.

MOLESTING OF GIRLS

Many girls have been molested by their father during their childhood and teens and great bitterness and resentment results. Spirits of frigidity, fear and other things take hold because of these incidents. Similarly, following marriage break-ups, children often have a tremendous sense of rejection.

I recall an incident when a woman came to me suffering from a major physical ailment and the Holy Spirit indicated that this problem related to her relationship with her grandfather. She was puzzled for a moment and then suddenly the memory flooded back to her because I mentioned the age of eight years. She recalled that when she was eight her grandfather had caused her to touch him physically on his private parts and her abhorrence of this sin was so great that it never left her mind. As she forgave her grandfather, the demon of resentment and bitterness left her and she walked away totally healed because that spirit of bitterness and resentment went at the same time with the physical infirmity.

FORGIVING A FATHER

When we were ministering near Seattle recently, at a Men's Advance, I taught in the area of deliverance. After the session, I heard a great noise coming from an adjacent room. I went in there to find five men trying to hold down a very tall young man who was extremely violent and who was, in fact, trying to pull out the windows of the building. I told the men to release this young man and as I took authority in the name of Jesus, the Holy Spirit told me to ask the young man about his father. Immediately, all the contortions and noise stopped and this twentyfour year old man broke down and wept like a little child.

It appeared that his father had deserted his family when he was six, and as a result, tremendous rejection and fear had entered the young boy who had grown into a man with these deep problems. He had sold his soul to Satan, hence the violent demonic powers which were operating through him.

As he began to forgive his father, the demons manifested violently. He was truly repentant and the demon of hate left him with a loud roar. He was immediately transformed as a person and when I last heard of him he was continuing strongly with the Lord, and in fact was involved in the deliverance ministry himself.

It seems to be one of the features of the deliverance ministry that where people have received deliverance, they themselves often operate in this ministry at a later date, because they are aware of the forces which have left them and have a holy hatred towards these forces.

SEVENTEEN

Methods of Deliverance

There are various ways in which demons can be cast out of people. Either as a single method or as a combination of methods, I have found the following ways to be effective in my own ministry. I reiterate that it is most important that we understand the authority that we have been given as ministers and disciples of Jesus Christ. Unless we are thoroughly grounded in our spirit with that authority, we will not be successful in the deliverance ministry. We must recall the authority vested in us:

"... *All authority has been given to me in heaven and on earth.*

"*Go therefore and make disciples of all the nations, baptizing them in the name of the Father and of the Son and of the Holy Spirit.*" (Matt 28:18,19)

Without a certainty of that authority in our spirit we will never be successful.

While I am preaching, I find that many times the Holy Spirit gives me an authority which is beyond my natural understanding because, at all times, I thoroughly believe the Word of God. Accordingly, during the course of such preaching it is not uncommon for demons to manifest by people falling to the ground with animal-like spirits manifesting through them. I usually do such ministry out in the open because as I read the scriptures I find that Jesus did His ministry openly and in the synagogue and not in a corner. It is good to see the power of Satan defeated publicly.

Sometimes the spirit of fear seeks to bind the people, but I point out that it is only the spirit of fear and certainly not the Spirit of God and if they will begin to understand what it is, they themselves can stand against that fear. On the other hand, if such fear is going to scare people into heaven and away from a lost eternity, I would rather see them fearful and scared into heaven than complacently riding into hell.

There are one or two practical points which we should note in a deliverance session. Before praying for the person to be delivered we should of course, seek either through discernment by the Holy Spirit or from their own testimony, the area of problem in their life. This may require some time for counselling and prayer together. During the actual deliverance they may be either seated or standing. If it is a long deliverance it may be preferable to have them seated. On some occasions they need to get on their knees and repent before God, and deliverance may in fact take place while they are on their knees.

SUGGESTED AREAS OF COUNSELLING IN RESPECT OF PEOPLE WHO MAY BE SUBJECT TO DEMON ACTIVITY

1. Ensure that they repent from occult activity.
2. Check the area of forgiveness, with particular relevance to parents, relatives etc.
3. Ensure that they honour their parents.
4. Ensure that they have renounced all sexual sin, including abortion, adultery, etc.
5. Ensure that any occultic activity on the part of the parents and ancestors has been renounced and repented from. They should also forgive those people.
6. Ensure that their house is cleansed.
7. If they have been into any seance or similar activity you can be sure demon activity will manifest around them.
8. Ensure that they have renounced all forms of unbelief and made Jesus their LORD and Saviour.
9. Ensure that they are really repentant.

10. Some people like the sin they are involved in. While they ask to be delivered they really do not want to give up the particular sin. There must be a real desire to be free from smoking or from addiction to alcohol, or to be free from sexual sins. The Holy Spirit can set them free in an instant if they are really repentant.

In the deliverance ministry I have used the following methods, which I do not claim to be exhaustive but which I have found to be very helpful:

When praying for specific cases, I make sure that the demons are aware of my knowledge of the power and the name of Jesus Christ and of the power of the blood of Jesus. Before beginning any such ministry, however, I always endeavour to ensure that the person to be delivered understands the need for repentance from all sin.

1. I HAVE USED MY PRAYER LANGUAGE
When we pray in tongues, our spirit prays . . .

> "For if I pray in a tongue, my spirit prays, but my understanding is unfruitful." (1 Cor. 14:14)

As we are praying in tongues our spirit is praying with the help of the Holy Spirit and we are using an authority far beyond the understanding or knowledge of our natural mind. Accordingly, we are no longer fettered by our natural mind. The language we are speaking may well be a known language, and certainly would be known to the demons. They can clearly understand that, with the help of the Holy Spirit we are praying with real authority to God and invoking His help. As we press in, unfettered by any natural doubts which would attack our carnal mind, demons begins to flee.

This, when spoken with full belief, will often provoke major manifestations on the part of the demons and eventually they will leave as we continue to press on in our prayer language. In fact, the way in which I came into the fluency in my prayer language was in praying this way for several hours with a person during the early part of my ministry, and as this person was delivered so my fluency improved.

2.   USE OF THE WORD OF GOD

It is good to quote scriptures with belief to those who are subject to demon power. The following are favourite scriptures of mine:

> "For God so loved the world that he gave his only begotten Son, that whoever believes in him should not perish but have everlasting life." (John 3:16)

> "And they were all filled with the Holy Spirit and began to speak with other tongues, as the Spirit gave them utterance." (Acts 2:4)

> "In the beginning was the Word, and the Word was with God, and the Word was God." (John 1:1)

On occasions I also torment the demons with the

fact that they will face the second death, by quoting the scripture:

> *"Then Death and Hades were cast into the lake of fire. This is the second death."* (Rev.20:14)

Often the demons will scream, "I don't want to hear it, I don't want to hear it!" We know then that we have the victory as we press in, believing the Word of God.

3.   CONFESSION OF SINS

I find that as people confess their sins in accordance with James 5:14-16 and we anoint them with oil, the demons manifest and disappear:

> *"Is anyone among you sick? Let him call for the elders of the church, and let them pray over him, anointing him with oil in the name of the Lord.*
>
> *And the prayer of faith will save the sick, and the Lord will raise him up. And if he has committed sins, he will be forgiven.*
>
> *Confess your trespasses to one another, and pray for one another, that you may be healed. The effective, fervent prayer of a righteous man avails much."* (James 5:14-16)

I find this particularly effective as I anoint with oil and speak slowly the words, "In the name of the Father, and of the Son, and of the Holy Spirit." As I believe and say these words with all my heart, the demons will scream and leave the person.

4. PRAISE GOD.

Another wonderful method of deliverance is praising God. I will often ask the person being delivered to simply say the words, "Praise God". They may say it up to fifty times before the demons scream and say they won't praise God, but then we know we have the victory and as the person presses on they are set free.

We know, of course, the reason for all of this, namely that God lives in the praises of His people, and as we praise God the Spirit of God comes down and drives out the demon power.

"But you are holy,
Who inhabit the praises of Israel." (Psalm 22:3)

Sometimes we must have the person repeat praising for a great number of times before it seems to enter deep into their spirit and dislodge the demon. On occasions, I have found that even the demon voice will use the words "Praise God", especially if they are demons of hidden anger. However, one can immediately tell that it is not the person themselves but the demon voice which is speaking. As we carry on and encourage the person to speak more and more, the demon finally cannot stand using the words, "Praise God". However, demons of deception are often so great that they will go along with the idea of using the words "Praise God" until they can stand it no longer and will scream in anger.

5. COMMANDING WITH AUTHORITY

We know that on several occasions, Jesus simply commanded the demons to go. He knew He had authority over them and He has given us that same authority. Here again, if we speak the Word of God with authority as a disciple of Jesus, and command the demon to go then it will leave the person.

A simple command to a demon to "Go" will always be effective when the demon knows that you are aware that you are acting under God's authority through Jesus Christ. You do not need to use lengthy phrases to command demons to leave but can simply command them to go, and if we do so with authority they will begin to leave.

6. REPENTANCE AND CONFESSIONS

Ensure the person has really repented and renounced all sin especially the sin of unbelief in the name of Jesus, confessing it, and calling on Jesus to save him or her.

It is fascinating to have demons manifest one after the other and to call them out one after the other, like a tangled skein, but unless there is real repentance on the part of the person being delivered it can all be in vain. At one time, I used to look for one demon after another, but I now realize that the key to all deliverance is true repentance. I now do not endeavour to call the demons out of the person until I have made sure that they have repented from their heart and then I know that true deliverance will take place.

I am, however, convinced that although we can spend much time speaking to and commanding many demons to leave a person, the final key is repentance. If the person is truly repentant in all the areas we have mentioned and renounces all sin, including that of his parents, and seeks the Lord with all his heart then the deliverance is made much easier. We can wear ourselves out commanding demons to leave a person, but unless there is real repentance in their heart the end result may be worse than the beginning.

Demons love to mock us and to show their power. We must always be aware that we have the authority in the name of Jesus and until we gain the upper hand it will mock us or hide, or do both. I remain firmly convinced that the quickest method of deliverance is true repentance on the part of the person involved. Even in cases which are as bad as schizophrenia, I believe there is a need for deep repentance in these cases.

There are many people who are obvious schizophrenics but others who are less obvious. In my own personal view, many more people than supposed are schizophrenic. Wherever there are two personalities (and this is very common) it is a case of schizophrenia. In these instances, deep repentance is required on the part of the true personality in order that the false personality, or personalities, are dismissed from what should be the temple of the Holy Spirit. True repentance means that the power of the Holy Spirit can become evident in the believer's life, and as soon as the false person realizes that the true person is gaining the upper hand, he will begin to leave with his hordes, even though there may be a great battle before the victory is finally won.

In the case of the schizophrenic, the prayers of the parents can be of immense value in breaking the hold that has come upon their children, no matter what their age may be. For this reason wherever possible, I go back to the parents and seek to counsel with them in such cases, so that they have a clear understanding of the nature of the battle.

7. CURSES AND SINS OF THE ANCESTORS

Ensure that the person has renounced the sins of their forefathers and forgiven their forefathers. We know from scripture that God visits the iniquities of the fathers on the children to the third and fourth generations of those who hate Him. (Exodus 20:5).

This is part of the curse of the law from which we were delivered through the cross of Jesus Christ, but we need to appropriate this deliverance by faith. In Galatians 3:13, we are told Chirst has redeemed us from the curse of the law, having become a curse for us.

In the same way the Word says that in order to be saved we need to be born again of the Spirit of God, not just having an intellectual acceptance of the Gospel. Indeed we must take hold of this promise of God and actually appropriate it. This is particularly true when there have been sins of previous generations.

I realize that there are various interpretations of the authority given by Jesus Christ to His disciples on the Sunday night of His resurrection concerning the forgiveness of sins:

> *"If you forgive the sins of any, they are forgiven them; if you retain the sins of any, they are retained."* (John 20:23)

Jesus Christ gave His disciples that authority to forgive or retain sins. This authority was only given when they had received the Spirit and were born again of the Spirit of God.

Many people hold on to the sins of their forefathers including their parents and take them into themselves thus binding themselves with those sins.

When we are born again of the Spirit of God, then we have the same authority. Accordingly, when we let go, or forgive, our ancestors or parents for any sin that they committed, we find that there is a complete cutting off from the past. Accordingly, I encourage people to repent for and forgive their ancestors, and as they exercise this forgiveness through the authority given by

Jesus Christ, the demons go.

I usually lead people in a prayer such as this "I John Smith repent from the sins of my forefathers and I specifically renounce those sins. I forgive my forefathers in the name of Jesus Christ". So much of these spiritual forces can come down through the seed. I often make the sign of the cross in front of the person. I do this by asking them to place their hand upon their navel and then make the sign of the cross over that area of their body. As we invoke the blood of Jesus Christ and cut off the spiritual powers which have come down through the umbilical cord, then with true forgiveness in the heart of the person, there can be real deliverance from the sins of the ancestors.

There are two clear scriptural examples from the Old Testament showing repentance from the sins of the ancestors.

> "*Please let your ear be attentive and your eyes open, that you may hear the prayer of your servant which I pray before you now, day and night, for the children of Israel your servants, and confess the sins of the children of Israel which we have sinned against you. Both my Father's house and I have sinned.*
>
> "*We have acted very corruptly against you, and have not kept the commandments, the statutes, nor the ordinances which you commanded your servant Moses".* (Nehemiah 1:6,7)
>
> "*Now while I was speaking, praying, and confessing my*

sin and the sin of my people Israel, and presenting my supplication before the Lord my God for the holy mountain of my God." (Daniel 9:20)

In order to be set free from the power of any curses whether from God, Man or from satanic influences or where they are self imposed, it is important to remember the following points and act upon them.

1. God promises blessings to those who diligently obey his voice and observe his commandments (Deuteronomy 28:1-13).

It is vital therefore that we obey the Lord our God, particularly his commandments

". . . You shall love the Lord your God with all your heart, with all your soul, with all your strength, and with all your mind, and your neighbour as your-self." (Luke 10:27)

"A new commandment I give to you, that you love one another; as I have loved you, that you also love one another." (John 13:34)

We should accordingly examine our hearts and be sure that this is our position with God and decide to fully obey God in all of these areas?

2. Confess Jesus Christ as our Lord and Saviour.

3. Confess all our sins as set out above particularly in respect of our family and ancestors.

4. Forgive everybody.

5. Renounce all contact with the occult and repent from any involvement on the part of our ancestors.
6. Accept, that in accordance with Galatians (Chapter 3:13 & 14). Jesus has delivered us from the curse. Believe this is so and confess that it is so.

By way of guidance only I would suggest a simple prayer as follows.

> *"Dear Heavenly Father I come to you in the name of Jesus Christ, I praise you Father and I worship you. I confess that Jesus Christ is my Lord and my Saviour. I confess that I have sinned and I also confess the sins of my ancestors known and unknown and renounce all of those sins and I renounce the gods of my ancestors, I repent from those sins and from all occultic activity on the part of my ancestors, I forgive my ancestors and I believe that on the cross Jesus Christ delivered me from the curse of the Law. And believe that I have been released from all curses through the name and through the blood of Jesus Christ."*

We have already pointed out that we have been delivered from the power of the curse, and one way for the person to appropriate that is to forgive and repent from the sins of their ancestors. However, there can be a spirit of curse present which has caused frequent accidents, suicides and death, and as we discern the spirit we need to take authority over it and command it to leave in the name of Jesus Christ. I well recall praying with parents of a six months' old baby where the child did not appear to be seeing anything at all. As we prayed against the spirit of curse which had come down on the father's side, and which had also affected the mother through the womb, then finally prayed for the child, there was an immediate change which took place within the child. He immediately began to look around and recognize people. It was quite apparent that, although his eyes were not physically blind, there was some form of spiritual and physical curtain affecting him. As the power of the curse was broken, the spirit left him.

8. KNOW THE ANOINTING OF THE HOLY SPIRIT.

One of the most powerful ways of seeing people delivered in the deliverance ministry is, I have found, to know the anointing of the Holy Spirit. Just as the oil was poured over Aaron to consecrate him as a priest and it ran over his head and down his beard as a type of the Holy Spirit, so indeed we can know that similar and warm anointing of the Holy Spirit because we are all kings and priests:-

"But you are a chosen generation, a royal priesthood, a holy nation, his own special people, that you may proclaim the praises of him who called you out of darkness into his marvellous light;" (1 Peter 2:9)

The anointing breaks the yoke.

"It shall come to pass in that day
That his burden will be taken away from your shoulder,

And his yoke from your neck,
And the yoke will be destroyed because of the anointing
oil." (Isa. 10.27)

I usually ask Jesus to pour down His anointing by the Holy Spirit and when I sense it falling I command the demon to go. Sometimes, when it is a particularly stubborn demon I call for a further portion of the anointing and as it falls I say to the demon, "Feel that anointing, demon". It invariably trembles and goes. Demons cannot stand the anointing of the Holy Spirit because through it they recognize our priestly authority in Jesus Christ.

BLOCKAGES TO THE ANOINTING

We will never know the anointing of the Holy Spirit if we ourselves have been involved in any occultic activity. Involvement in any occultic activity such as Freemasonry, horoscopes, hypnotism, etc., will quench the power of the Holy Spirit as another spirit is resting upon us. Until we totally renounce this sin, either on our own part or on the part of our parents, we shall not know the anointing of the Holy Spirit. We can often feel that anointing pouring right down through ourselves, particularly through our arms, and as we lay hands on the person the anointing touches them and the demons begin to flee.

OCCULT

It is vital that the person to whom we are ministering

renounces any involvement in the occult and for this reason you will find a list in Appendix 1. concerning all forms of the occult. It is good to ask people to go through the list and tick those areas in which they have been involved so that they can be specifically renounced.

In renouncing particular sins, it is useful for the person to use their full name, such as, "I, James Peter Bond renounce in Jesus' name the sin of witchcraft. I confess that sin in Jesus' name and call on You, Lord Jesus, to help me." There seems to be some additional power involved when the person themselves, by using their full name, causes the spirit to go.

9. WATER BAPTISM.

If the person has not undergone water batism at some stage in their life, then this is a powerful way of cutting off the old man and the demon powers and we should ensure that, after proper tuition such persons can expect deliverance in water baptism

10. BAPTISM IN THE HOLY SPIRIT.

If there is one thing to which the demons object, it is the person surrendering their tongue to the Holy Spirit and receiving a Holy Spirit tongue. This is part of the infilling process of the Holy Spirit and allows Him to occupy the temple of the Holy Spirit in its entirety.

Sometimes demons will sit on the person's tongue and give what appears to be a Holy Spirit language whereas it is in fact a demonic language. We need to be able to discern this. The person seems to lose control of what they are saying and go into a kind of trance in those circumstances, and we need to be able to discern that this is not a Holy Spirit tongue but a demonic tongue. I usually get such people to renounce all sin and then ask them to start again in their Holy Spirit tongue. They may need to start several times because each time they start and say a few words one can discern the demonic tongue coming again. As the person grows stronger in their Holy Spirit tongue the demon tongue dies down and finally goes altogether. Yes, baptism in the Holy Spirit is one of the most powerful ways of getting people delivered from demon power.

11. LISTENING TO THE HOLY SPIRIT

As we grow in faith, in the word of knowledge and word of wisdom we can hear the Holy Spirit directing us as to how we should pray.

When I am praying, I find that the Holy Spirit specifically directs me as to how I should pray. Sometimes He tells me to command the demon to leave in His name, and at the same time directs how I should place my hands on the person's body. Sometimes I place my hand on their neck, on the back of their head, or on the top of their head or on their forehead, or on their eyes, or on their nose. Sometimes, it is on their throat.

Usually you will find that if you are directed to such a

position on the person's body that they often have pain attached to that part of the body and they receive deliverance as the demon goes.

If you are directed to pray in respect of the person's chest or stomach or other parts of the body, I always ask the person to place their hands on that part of the body first and then I lay my hand on their hands. We must be very careful and do all things properly, particularly when we are praying for women.

THE ATTACK BY DEMONS ON US.

Sometimes when we are ministering, a demon will seek to attack us in a specific way. For example, many times when I am praying with women, the demon of lust will leave their body and attack me in the sexual area. We must keep our minds absolutely pure and wholesome as we are praying, otherwise we give entry to such a spirit. When we stand firm on the Word of God and know the protection of His blood and the anointing of the Holy Spirit, the demon realises that it cannot enter us. Sometimes after a prolonged deliverance or a strong preaching session, I have woken up in the early hours of the morning to feel an oppressive weight on me and almost a delicious feeling as energy is sucked out of me. I lie there wondering what is happening and suddenly realize it is a demon. I have commanded it to leave in Jesus' name and immediately it has gone.

We must be aware that Satan will seek to attack us if

he possibly can, but we must stand firm on the power of the Holy Spirit within us.

12. MINISTER SELF ACCEPTANCE

One of the entry points for demon activity is the failure of people to accept themselves. Ephesians 1:6 says that we are, "accepted in the Beloved". God accepted us while we were still sinners by allowing Jesus to die on the cross for us and therefore people should realize and be taught that God accepts them. This is a great release point for many people.

I recall one man who came to me many times after my meetings and demons manifested each time I prayed. They seem to live everywhere in him. When I prayed, there was a real measure of deliverance but he seemed to come back the following week or month with the same problem. One night I told him that Jesus loved him. He looked at me in stunned silence and then began to weep and said, "Do you really mean that Jesus loves me?" I told him that this is exactly what the Holy Spirit had told me to say to him a moment or two earlier. He sat down and wept. The entry point of demon activity in his life had been the failure to accept himself. He felt that God had rejected him even though the scriptures taught him otherwise. As self-acceptance was ministered to him, he received his deliverance. When people are taught that God accepts and loves them, then they should also be taught to accept themselves. Failure to accept oneself again provides a major entry point for demon activity.

13. FASTING

This can be a powerful weapon in deliverance as long as it is done with the correct motives. Let us not fast wrongly as set out as follows (Isaiah 58:3,4)

> *"Why have we fasted", they say,*
> *"and you have not seen?*
> *Why have we afflicted our souls,*
> *And You take no notice?"*
> *"In fact, in the day of your fast*
> *you find pleasure,*
> *And exploit all your labourers.*
> *Indeed you fast for strife and debate,*
> *And to strike with the fist of wickedness."*

If fasting is done for the right motives it brings us into a new spiritual dimension. I often commend fasting on the part of the person who is seeking deliverance and counsel them in the area of repentance. Fasting seems to bring our spirit alive and open our spirit to the power of the Holy Spirit. On occasions, the person ministering should also fast, particularly in a difficult case, as this will stir the power of the Holy Spirit within him.

I recently ministered to a pastor who had experienced great problems in his early life before he turned to Jesus Christ. There was still a powerful demon affecting his life and I encouraged him to fast for twenty-four hours before I prayed with him. When I did come to pray for him, the Lord gave me a vision showing the root of the tree having been cut when this man was water baptized, but that the vine was still attached to the walls of his flesh. It was still feeding off the flesh. When he fasted, the vine began to lose its hold on the walls of his flesh (so to speak) and deliverance was accomplished.

During the course of this particular deliverance, the principal demon screamed out that he had hated the fasting which the pastor had undergone. This, I believe, clearly showed that, while water baptism can cut the root, sometimes there are still hooks in the flesh in which the demons live and which need to be totally cut off by fasting and seeking God.

14. BREATHING

I often commend people to inhale sharply and believe they are breathing in the Holy Spirit and then breathe out, or expel the demon power within them. The Holy Spirit often indicates to me that the demon power is coming out of their stomach up into their chest and into their throat, and then out of the mouth. Sometimes I see this manifested in my spirit as a fish or a serpent coming out of the person's mouth . . . first the head, then the stomach, and finally the tail.

This technique of course is perfectly scriptual for Jesus Christ said in Mark's Gospel these words.

"... *In my name they will cast out (expel) demons;"* (*Mark* 16:17)

As people breathe out sharply they in fact can expel the demons in this way. Sometimes breathing will start on an involuntary basis when the demons realize they must go. On one occasion, a person challenged me as to the validity of this form of deliverance. The next night at one of the meetings the same person began to manifest a spirit in front of me. She began to breathe in sharply and breathe out on an involuntary basis and a powerful demon manifested itself as though it had been the demon of unbelief which had been questioning me the night before as to this form of deliverance.

We must be careful not to categorize or fall into standard methods of deliverance. We must always be open to the power of the Holy Spirit. What will work on one occasion will not necessarily work on another occasion. We must be open to a combination of methods of deliverance, but I do find that the breathing technique is an excellent one on many occasions.

15. BLOCKING ENTRY POINT

The navel is often an entry point for demon power which have come down through the umbilical cord before birth, or at birth. Demons have told me that they have entered through the seed of the male into the female and then down through the umbilical cord into the person to whom I am ministering. Frequently, with the permission of the person, I place my hand over that part of their body (after they have placed their own hands on it) and command the demon power to be cut off in Jesus' name, often with powerful results.

Sometimes under the direction of the Holy Spirit I take hold of the person's hands and command the spirit which is bothering them to come out. Quite frequently spirits come out through a person's hands. the spirit of masturbation often manifests by the fingers moving backwards and forwards. However, we must not assume that, because this happens, that the person has been involved in that particular sin. Sometimes the hands twist into a peculiar shape as demon powers leave the person.

16. AGREEMENT

A powerful method of deliverance is for the parties praying to agree for that deliverance. We have the authority of the Word of God in this respect:

> "Assuredly, I say to you, whatever you bind on earth will be bound in heaven, and whatever you loose on earth will be loosed in heaven.
> "Again I say to you that if two of you agree on earth concerning anything that they ask, it will be done for them by my Father in heaven.

"For where two or three are gathered together in my name, I am there in the midst of them." (Matthew 18:18-20)

It is necessary for the parties agreeing to absolutely harmonize in their spirit and totally agree for the person's deliverance. As the principal demon senses that agreement and obedience to the Word of God, he will loose his grip and take with him subordinate demons.

I stress that there must be complete agreement in the spirit before deliverance will be accomplished in this way.

17. USE OF WATER

On various occasions I have found that when water is blessed and then applied to the person seeking deliverance, there can be a real release from demon power. On such occasions I have reminded the demon that the person has been water baptized. The use of water in this way reminds the person that during their baptism they were cut-off from the power of sin in their life. As this is acknowledged the demon power flees.

18. CLEANSING OF HOUSES

Sometimes the person's home needs to be cleansed. We have previously spoken of the need to remove all objects which may have any occultic significance. As we use scriptures and plead the blood of Jesus over every room, the demon powers will flee. On some occasions, I have found that the Holy Spirit has directed me to place my hands on each corner of the house, particularly near the foundations. In this way, by taking authority in the name of Jesus Christ and invoking the power of the blood of Jesus, there has been a total release of demon power from those houses.

On some occasions, I have been asked by the clergy to participate in cleansing a church from demon power and in the same way the Holy Spirit has encouraged me to lay my hands upon each corner of the church building, as well as commanding the spirits to leave from within the building.

19. FINDING THE LEADER OF THE PACK.

With the help of the Holy Spirit we need to seek out the leader of the demon powers within a person. We must be aware that he will often send out all the other demons but he himself will not depart. We must seek the gift of discernment in this area.

It is important to find the strong man, whatever he may be called. Very frequently I find the strong man is the Jezebel spirit referred to earlier, as well as the Antichrist and Death and Hell spirits. As these are particularly strong men it is good to have others pray with you while you agree that these spirits must leave. On other occasions, the strong man will simply be the demon of lust or fornication or hatred, bitterness, or resentment, but whatever he is, we must seek him out and ensure that because we see manifestations he is not simply sending the other demons out while he himself remains within.

Demons seem to operate in various clusters and on occasions we can find that a demon with the same name can be present in several clusters. We therefore need not be concerned to find that when we have cast out a spirit of lust, another spirit of lust names itself. He has related to a separate cluster in the same person.

This same principle can operate in respect of other spirits.

20. LAYING ON OF HANDS

It is absolutely scriptural to lay hands on people during the course of deliverance. Jesus did so.

In Luke 4:39 we see that Jesus "rebuked the fever". He thus dealt with the fever as a demon. Similarly in Matthew 8:15 we find, "And he touched her hand, and the fever left her . . . "

Again, there was the women who was bowed down by the spirit of infirmity:

> "And behold, there was a woman who had a spirit of infirmity eighteen years, and was bent over and could in no way raise herself up.
> But when Jesus saw her, he called her to him and said to her, "Woman, you are loosed from your infirmity."
> And he laid his hands on her, and immediately she was made straight, and glorified God." (Luke 13:11-13)

As we lay hands on people with the authority of Jesus Christ in the deliverance ministry, we will find that the power of God surges through our body and touches the person for whom we are praying. They sense the anointing of God and the demon powers begin to leave.

21. PRAYER BY THE PERSON BEING DELIVERED CALLING ON JESUS TO HELP THEM

It is good that the person being delivered repents from sin and confesses the name of Jesus and calls on Jesus to help them. The following simple prayer can be extremely effective, if it is believed in the heart:

> "Dear heavenly Father, I come to You in the name of Jesus Christ. I come a sinner. I confess my sins and I repent of them. I am sorry that I have sinned. I believe that You sent Jesus Christ into this world, born of a virgin, in the flesh, as a man. I believe that Jesus Christ died on the cross to cleanse me from sin. I believe that He was my substitute to satisfy God's justice for sin. I believe that Jesus Christ, by His death on the cross, gave me the gift of eternal life and the gift of right-standing with You, dear heavenly Father. He gave me healing for my body, soul and spirit. I believe that He was buried but that He rose again on the third day in accordance with the scriptures and is seated now at the right hand of God.
>
> I turn to you, Lord Jesus, I turn away from all darkness, from the power of Satan to the power of God, and I renounce all the works of Satan, especially the occult. I call out to you, Lord Jesus, to help me. I ask You to be my Lord and Saviour. I believe that You are my Deliverer, and

*that through your death and resurrection I have been
delivered from the power of the devil. Thank you, Jesus. I
believe I am being saved, I believe I am healed, I believe I
am delivered."*

22. PLEADING THE BLOOD OF JESUS CHRIST

As we know there is great power in the blood of
Jesus Christ. During deliverance sessions I often
encourage people to repeat what are known as the
blood scriptures set out in Appendix 2. As they repeat
them one at a time with belief, demon power will often
manifest. The demon hates the person to confess the
Word of God.

I go through these scriptures one at a time and
encourage the person to repeat them after me. If the
Holy Spirit shows me that one of these scriptures is
dealing with a particular bondage in a person's life, for
example, that they do not realise that they have been
forgiven then I ask them to repeat the scripture dealing
with forgiveness a number of times until I am sure that
they are set free. It is the confession through their
mouth and belief in their heart which sets them free
and drives the demon power out. I strongly commend
the use of these scriptures as set out in Appendix 2.
during all deliverance sessions.

23. ASSERTION OF THE PERSON'S WILL

It is imperative that the person asserts their own will
during deliverance. By that I mean that as the demon

manifests through them the person can become passive and let this happen. They must be encouraged to exercise their will in standing against the demon power. As they exercise their will in conjunction with the Holy Spirit within them then the demon power will begin to lose its hold and finally leave. We have previously quoted the scriptual basis for this, namely.

"You are of God, little children, and have overcome them, because he who is in you is greater than he who is in the world." (1 John 4:4)

24. ANGELS OF PROTECTION

On many occasions as I have been ministering in deliverance, I have realized that we have the ministering angels in accordance with Hebrews 1:14 surrounding us. I well remember on one occasion when a person to whom I was ministering was manifesting violently in my study. Suddenly, he turned towards the window and pointed to the outside of my property and the demon began to scream in a loud voice, "They are everywhere, they are everywhere!" I thought at that time that he was referring to other demons near our house. The person was violently trembling, as the demon caused him to do so.

Some days later, the Lord reminded me of the incident and told me that they were angels of protection surrounding my house. A few months later, a similar incident occurred. On that occasion, and in the same way, another person was being ministered to and suddenly that person turned towards the window and the demon began to scream through him, "They are everywhere, they are everywhere!" I was able to say to the demons, "Yes, they are angels ... God's angels", and the demon voice replied, "Yes, yes, yes." The demon was obviously terrified.

It is most reassuring to know that we have the presence of God's angels around us as we fight these spiritual battles.

25. FOLLOW UP

It is important that those who have received deliverance are followed up by ministers of the gospel, preferably their own pastors or somebody who can minister to them and they should be prayed for regularly. If they slip back into the old sin, or if pride enters, then there can be powerful deception.

EIGHTEEN

Self Deliverance

Some people ask whether they can be delivered by themselves.

This is completely possible if there is faith on the part of the person who is expecting deliverance. This faith must of course be grounded in Jesus Christ. In addition however, it is usually necessary to have the gift of discernment of spirits because we need to know what spirits are attacking us.

If it is simply of oppression then we can of course command it to go.

"Therefore submit to God.
Resist the devil and he will flee from you." (James 4:7)

I have at times woken up in the night to find a heavy oppression upon me or even a spirit of suffocation. I have realized that something is pressing down upon me and I have commanded it to go in the name of Jesus Christ and have found that it has lifted and gone. Similarly we can have feelings of panic or fear which grip us and we can command them to leave. Sometimes the Holy Spirit will direct us to the part of the body upon which we should lay our hands such as our eyes or ears.

As a person under authority in Jesus Christ we have the power to resist the devil. There is however another side to the coin. Sometimes people believe they are delivered when in fact they are not. This is why we need to be part of the body of Christ and submit to other members in the body of Christ particularly those who have discernment in these areas of spirits. In this way he can be "checked out".

The same basic principles apply to self deliverance as to any other form of deliverance namely there must be true repentance and confession of sin as well as forgiveness and breaking with any form of the occult. We must know our authority in Jesus Christ in order to command the spirits to leave us. If we do not have peace or know that we are still under affliction and bondage we should certainly seek immediate help from those qualified to give it.

We must always be certain that our desire for self deliverance is not based on pride, namely that we do not want others to know that we have a problem and that we are unwilling to confess it before them. If this is the basis of seeking self deliverance then we will not find the relief which we seek.

I find self deliverance particularly helpful in the case of pain or sickness attacking my body. As I place my hand on the part of my body afflicted and command the spirit of sickness or pain to leave and believe for healing then I find that the Lord ministers to me mightily.

The other important area of self deliverance involves the person who has already undergone deliverance with the help of others. After the ministry has finished, the person may well find that there are still demons attacking him or her. That person needs to be counselled concerning their ability to resist the devil and to stand against these forces that are attacking them. When I have prayed for a person for deliverance I am always wary of telling them that they are completely delivered. The evidence of complete deliverance may not appear for several days because demon powers could still be leaving the person over the next few days as that person stands against them.

It is particularly important to advise people that they have the power of the Holy Spirit within them to resist demons. If they are not counselled in this way, they will always be seeking help from others, whereas by exercising their own will with the help of the Holy Spirit within them, they can defeat these demon powers.

NINETEEN

Possessing The Land

There is a scriptural principle which we need to grasp in the areas of deliverance and healing. We find that when God was encouraging His people to enter the promised land, He did not say that He would give them that land in one moment of time:

"And I will send hornets before you, which shall drive out the Hivite, the Canaanite, and the Hittite from before you.

"I will not drive them out from before you in one year, lest the land become desolate and the beast of the field become too numerous for you.

"Little by little I will drive them out from before you, until you have increased, and you inherit the land.

"And I will set your bounds from the Red Sea to the Sea of the Philistines, and from the desert to the River. For I will deliver the inhabitants of the land into your hand, and you shall drive them out before you.

"*You shall make no covenant with them, nor with their gods.*

"*They shall not dwell in your land, lest they make you sin against me. For if you serve their gods, it will surely be a snare to you.*" (Exodus 23:28-33)

POSSESS THE LAND

We always need to encourage people to "possess the land" which they have taken from the enemy through deliverance and healing. The enemy must be driven out of these areas of our lives and sometimes people are disappointed when they realize they have not obtained complete deliverance in one session. They need to be built up upon the Word and in their faith in Jesus Christ. Accordingly I always point out to people who have taken land from the enemy that they should hold on to it while he counter-attacks. As they take thorough control of the ground that they have been given, then they will grow in faith and be able to take more land from the enemy.

We live in an era of "instant tea, instant coffee" and people want "instant deliverance and healing". Sometimes this is accomplished, but on most occasions we must hold on to that part of the land which we have taken from the enemy and consolidate our position. Then we will be able to entirely conquer him.

DELIVERANCE CAN BE PROGRESSIVE

For how long should we minister?

Sometimes there can be a prolonged deliverance ministry required for a person. In such cases, I have come to learn, it is good to minister for a period and see demons released, but I always counsel the person to go away, read their Word, get on their knees before the Lord, confess their sins, and come into true repentance. I also counsel them to be baptized in the Holy Spirit. If they will do these things then they can come back a week or two later, and you will find that they have progressed considerably in the power of the Holy Spirit and are in a much stronger position to resist the demons which are seeking to inhabit them. In this way, two things are accomplished:

Firstly, we do not become so exhausted physically that we cannot face further deliverance sessions.

Secondly, the person grows in true repentance and knowledge of the Lord.

Satan delights to confront us with people who are so bound with demons that we become utterly exhausted and are not able to continue ministering to other people.

SELFISHNESS

Remember also, that there is a streak of selfishness in most of us, and some people will continue to seek ministry from others rather than repent. Whether they are going to secure permanent deliverance will largely rest upon their reaction to such advice as going away and repenting. If they are not prepared to do so then you can be wasting your time in casting demons out of them because they will still leave themselves open through bitterness, resentment, pride, hate, and other fleshly aspects, to further demon activity.

Just as physical healing can be progressive in many cases, in the same way deliverance can also be progressive.

Often times, real healing must take place in a marriage before full deliverance is effected and this may require constant prayer for the other partner to be brought to the Lord so that the demonic activity which is constantly attacking the remaining partner will go.

We are told by Jesus to love our enemies, bless those who curse us and do good to those who hate us:

> "But I say to you, love your enemies, bless those who curse you, do good to those who hate you, and pray for those who spitefully use you and persecute you." (Matt. 5:44)

In this way I often get people to pray for the person who may have broken up their marriage. As a blessing is prayed on that person, the spirit of torment, which is coming from that person and afflicting the innocent spouse, retires in confusion and God's spirit of love comes through the person who is praying the prayer with belief.

TWENTY

Why People Are Not Delivered

1. They do not repent.

There is not a real turning from sin in their heart nor the desire to really repent from their sins. They are not ready to give up sin and make Jesus Lord and Saviour of their lives.

Many people know Jesus as the Messiah but not as Lord of every part of their life. Until they make Him Lord of their thought life, their emotions, their sexual desires, and every part of their being, they will not be set free.

When we are ministering to people, we need to show the full love of Jesus Christ. We must not be judgmental but continue to exhibit that love at all times and let the love flow through us, so that God's anointing can in turn minister through us.

In the area of repentance, we therefore need to have not only love but a discernment as to whether the person has really repented and does not feel just remorseful. There is a great difference between repentance and remorse. Repentance is actually turning from the sin and making a decision of the will, whereas remorse is being sorry that one has sinned. Judas was remorseful, he did not repent.

2. THEY FAIL TO CONFESS SPECIFIC SINS.

Especially the sins of adultery and abortion, with the result that these spirits are still attached to them and they cannot be set free.

ABORTION

Abortion is a very deep sin as it is the same thing as murder when the abortion is voluntary. Tremendous spirits of guilt follow after an abortion. Guilt, fear, resentment, hurt, and many other spirits enter with abortion. Many women are reluctant to confess that they have had an abortion and they may require separate counselling away from their husbands because it could have occurred before their marriage. Until this is thoroughly repented of, there will be no deliverance. In those cases it is necessary to lay hands upon the womb of the woman in order to have complete deliverance. As stated earlier when ministering to a woman, I am always very careful where I lay hands on the front portion of her body. I always ask her to lay hands first on that part of the body and then I lay my hand over it. I frequently find that there is sickness in the area of the womb or stomach as a result of abortion, and as the spirit of abortion departs, the sickness also leaves.

3. THEY FAIL TO FORGIVE

This has been discussed very fully. Failure to forgive means that Satan still has a right to be involved with that person and will not depart until true forgiveness takes place. In some cases it will be necessary for the person to make restitution, such as going to see the person who has hurt them and telling that person they forgive them, or asking forgiveness of a person against whom they themselves have held resentment.

4. FAILURE TO BREAK WITH THE OCCULT AND FALSE RELIGIONS.

Unless there is an absolute break with the occult, such as destroying all occultic books, and any heathen figures in their homes such as Buddhas, or anything which is being, or has been, used for demon worship or any statues or carvings, then the spirit will remain in their home and continue to attack them.

There needs to be a complete renouncing of the occult. It may be necessary to take the person through the list in Appendix 1. of this book and ask them to nominate those forms of the occult in which they have been involved and specifically renounce this specific area of the occult. Until this takes place they will never be set free. Again, those who have been involved in Freemasonry must destroy every vestige of their regalia or other belongings which they received during their involvement in Freemasonry.

To sum up there must be a complete and absolute repudiation and renunciation of everything occultic.

5. FAILURE TO REPENT FROM PRIDE.

Pride can be an entry point for all forms of demon activity and of course it was pride which led to Satan's fall. There must be a real humbling of oneself before God and repentance from all pride, if there is to be true deliverance.

6. CIRCUMSTANCES

Frequently, the fact that they are living in a home where there is unbelief or great sin will make it very difficult for the person to retain their deliverance. They need to ensure that they are associating with strong Christians in a strong fellowship so that the demon powers in their home can be bound.

The wife who has an unbelieving husband must remember that the unbelieving husband is sanctified by the wife, and similarly in the case where the husband has an unbelieving wife, he must remember that he sanctifies his wife. (1 Corinthians 7:14). Otherwise their children would be unclean.

As we understand the power of the Holy Spirit

operating within us, even though our partner is an unbeliever, the Holy Spirit will completely protect us.

7. FAILURE ON THE PART OF THE PARENTS
   TO REPENT

I have seen cases where a mother has entered into true repentance and a daughter living at home has lapsed back into her problems because, although the father has made a form of commitment, he has refused to continue in full repentance with the Lord. The same demon powers which entered through him and affected the daughter in her younger life, still have a foothold and regain a stronghold in the daughter's life. We must remember that unless there is a complete cutting off from sin in these situations and true repentance, the doorway is still open for attack on members of the family.

How Do We Know When We Are Delivered?

For those of us who are suffering from physical infirmity, which has been caused by demons, such as arthritis, headaches, pain or some addiction such as smoking, or alcohol, we will know when we are delivered. There will be no doubt in our mind because we will have felt the demon go and we will know our physical improvement.

Again, with spirits of oppression we will feel completely free when they have gone. Let us remember, however, the words of Jesus:-

> "When an unclean spirit goes out of a man, he goes through dry places, seeking rest, and finds none.
>
> "Then he says, 'I will return to my house from which I came.' And when he comes, he finds it empty, swept, and put in order.
>
> "Then he goes and takes with him seven other spirits

more wicked than himself, and they enter and dwell there;
and the last state of that man is worse than the first. so
shall it also be with this wicked generation." (Matt.
12:43-45)

REFILL HOUSE

If we do not ensure that the house is totally filled
with the Holy Spirit and we are totally surrendered to
the Lord, there is a danger of the demons re-entering.

In other cases, where demon activity has been less
pronounced or more subtle, such as in the case of
rejection, fear, anger, depression we will also sense the
departure of demon activity. The great danger then is
for Christians to say that they are totally set free and
Satan gives them the impression that they are not
under attack on a future date.

We are engaged in spiritual warfare:

"For we do not wrestle against flesh and blood, but
against principalities, against powers, against the rulers of
the darkness of this age, against spiritual hosts of wicked-
ness in the heavenly places." (Eph. 6:12)

Satan will not leave us alone but will attempt to
throw darts at us at every opportunity. One of his chief
weapons is pride, followed by deception and rebellion.
It is therefore very important that we keep a humble
attitude at all times, remain open to the counsel of
others, particularly the members of the body of Christ,

and ensure that the FRUIT of the Holy Spirit is operating in our life.

THE OLD MAN

As the Apostle Paul said, we need to die daily, that is we need to place our old man on the cross and crucify him. Our old nature will seek to rise up in us and take over and with it the demon forces will try and re-enter. Old habits die hard. The old nature will seek to re-assert itself at every opportunity unless it is well and truly crucified. For example, the way in which we speak to other people, the way in which we relate to them, can be evidence as to whether the new nature has really taken hold within us . . . that is the new nature of Christ. If we remain unforgiving or hold wrong attitudes, then obviously the old nature is re-asserting itself and we are in danger of allowing demon activity to re-enter again.

Let us face it. The battle will continue until the very day that we go to be with the Lord. This is why I keep speaking of the need for daily repentance and the need daily to make Jesus Lord of every part of our life and to be continuously filled with the Holy Spirit. If we walk humbly and carefully before the Lord then the opportunity for Satan to attack us is greatly diminished and we can walk in true victory.

> "And do not be drunk with wine, in which is dissipation; but be filled with the Spirit,
> "speaking to one another in psalms and hymns and

*spiritual songs, singing and making melody in your heart
to the Lord.* (Eph. 5:18,19)

Let us remember and name clearly the lusts of the
flesh:

*"Now the works of the flesh are evident, which are:
adultery, fornication, uncleanness, licentiousness,*

*idolatry, sorcery, hatred, contentions, jealousies, out-
bursts of wrath, selfish ambitions, dissensions, heresies,*

*envy, murders, drunkenness, revels, and the like; of
which I tell you beforehand, just as I also told you in time
past, that those who practise such things will not inherit the
kingdom of God."* (Galatians 5:19-21)

"THE FLESH LUSTETH AGAINST THE SPIRIT AND THE SPIRIT AGAINST THE FLESH"

We must seek daily the fruit of the Holy Spirit to
operate in our lives as we yield to Jesus Christ, namely
love, joy, peace, longsuffering, kindness, goodness,
faithfulness, gentleness, self control, meekness, tem-
perance. When this fruit of the Holy Spirit is operating
and is flowering in our life, there is little opportunity for
demon activity to manifest.

Remember the scripture from 1 Peter:

*"If the righteous one is scarcely saved, Where will the
ungodly and the sinner appear?"* (1 Peter 4:18)

NARROW WAY

Yes, the way is a narrow way, and although many are
called, few are chosen because they do not allow Jesus

to be Lord of their lives. Many succumb to the old ways and go back into the world. While we are in the world we are not of the world, and although we must maintain an attitude of love at all times towards all people; let us not fall into the trap of becoming part of the world, thus allowing the spirit of Satan to gain ascendancy again in our lives.

Jesus has won the victory for us, but we must appropriate it, maintaining a daily holy walk with the Lord. We cannot do this in our own strength, only in the strength which the Holy Spirit gives. In this way we will know true joy and peace in our hearts.

When people enter our home, they should sense peace, the peace of the Holy Spirit in it. Where there is that peace, there is little opportunity for Satan to manifest his hatred and disruptive tactics.

Summing up then it must be a witness of the Spirit on the part of the person being delivered that they are indeed set free. They will know whether in fact the driving, compelling, tormenting demon has left and taking with it restlessness. Only God knows the true state of the person's heart and therefore it is a matter between that person and God himself.

I am careful about telling people that they are completely set free. I can certainly witness with them to their freedom from a particular demonic power with his host but that person must seek their assurance from God himself. If we are to precipitate in telling people that they are completely free then they could be blinded to other forces still present within them which have not gone.

It is good to remind a person that while the main demonic force has left with his hosts, there may be some demons still staying around waiting to re-enter or others which have still to leave. Therefore the person should keep their heart open before God in true repentance over the next few days, in particular, so that they can be sure of their deliverance in the expelling of any further demonic powers within them.

TWENTY TWO

Binding Demons When The Person Is Not Present

PRAYING FOR PEOPLE WHO ARE NOT PRESENT

I believe that we have the same authority referred to in the previous scriptures (Matt. 18:18-20) to bind and loose spirits which are afflicting other people who are not present. These spirits may be spirits of unbelief or doubt or procrastination, or any such spirit which is preventing a person hearing the voice of God and coming into full repentance. In such cases, I often agree with others, that we bind the spirit afflicting such a person even though they are not in our presence, then release the person from that spirit. In this way, we often find great miracles occurring among those who are not even with us.

I well recall a case where a particular person was constantly causing difficulty in a prayer meeting. It was quite apparent that he had a dominating spirit and wanted to control everything that took place. He would not receive counsel in this respect.

Three of the members of the prayer group went aside and bound the spirit that was speaking through that person without his knowledge. For the next six months, the person barely spoke at the prayer meetings and the Spirit of God was able to minister in a beautiful way, not only to him but also to the others present.

The three persons who had agreed to bind the spirit in that person became concerned, however, because he was not participating at all in the meetings, so they agreed to loose the spirit from him and then found that there was proper participation.

Let us remember the authority given to us by Jesus, namely:

> "... *Whatever you bind on earth will be bound in heaven, and whatever you loose on earth will be loosed in heaven.*"
>
> "*Again I say to you that if two of you agree on earth concerning anything that they ask, it will be done for them by my father in heaven.*
>
> "*For where two or three are gathered together in my name, I am there in the midst of them.*" (Matthew 18:18-20)

There are many circumstances where we cannot at that stage gain the assistance of the person whom we are seeking to have delivered. Let us not despair.

Remember the power that is in the Word of God and the promise of Jesus Christ.

> "Now this is the confidence that we have in him, that if we ask anything according to his will, he hears us". (1 John 5:14)

It is in accordance with God's will for people to be set free from demon power, so let us remember to pray with confidence in such instances.

Over the years, I have known of many parents praying for children who had disappeared, and from whom they have not heard for a long time. As they have bound the demon power affecting those children and have prayed in belief, the children have responded to them and full reconciliation has taken place.

I recall one case when we prayed for a young adult whose parents had not heard from her for a number of years. At that very moment somebody began to witness to that young person in a far-off country and she came to the Lord. She wrote to her parents and there was full reconciliation.

The spirits binding another person may be spirits of unbelief, doubt, procrastination or any spirit which is preventing a person from hearing the voice of God and coming into full repentance.

Never let us forget the power that is in the Word of God, and believe and act upon it. It is wonderful to know that this power is available to all who call upon the Lord Jesus Christ.

TWENTY THREE

Where Do Demons Go?

We know from scripture that when an unclean spirit leaves a man, he goes through dry places, seeking rest:

> "When an unclean spirit goes out of a man, he goes through dry places, seeking rest, and finds none." (Matt. 12:43)

I believe that Jesus had authority to cast demons into the pit:

> "And suddenly they cried out, saying, "What have we to do with you, Jesus, you Son of God? Have you come here to torment us before the time?" (Matt. 8:29)

It is clear that they knew that Jesus had authority to torment them before the final time when demon powers are cast in the lake of fire and brimstone.

> "And the devil, who deceived them, was cast into the lake of fire and brimstone where the beast and the false

prophet are. And they will be tormented day and night forever and ever." (Rev. 20:10)

On occasions, particularly in stubborn cases, I have told the demon that if he does not leave, I would send him to the pit. I believe that, as a disciple of Jesus Christ, I have that authority. You must, however, arrive at your own conclusion. On such an occasion, I have seen a great manifestation occur and the demon has left. However, in all of this, we must be guided by the Holy Spirit.

When we are praying in a public place, it is good to command the demons to go from the building and touch no person in that building. This gives confidence to those who are watching.

I know that on occasions, people send the demons to places of divine appointment. While this may be in order, I do not find any specific scriptural basis for it.

TWENTY FOUR

Exercise Of Will

As we have said earlier in this book, it is most imperative that people understand that they must exercise their will at all times. God has given us a will and normally He will not interfere with it. He expects us to exercise the authority He has given us, so that when we are being delivered, we need to understand how imperative it is that our will be exercised.

We can exercise our will for good or bad. When we exercise our will, we realize the truth of the scripture:

> "You are of God, little children, and have overcome them, because he who is in you is greater than he who is in the world." (1 John 4:4)

In this modern age, we have become so accustomed to obtaining results from pills and medicines without any active exercise of our own will, that it is often difficult for us to realize that we need to exercise our will in all areas of life under God's authority and according to the wisdom given by His Word.

It is thus imperative that we encourage people who are being delivered to recognize that God has given them a will and they have the authority to stand against the enemy.

WEALTHY YOUNG MAN

I well remember the case of a wealthy young man who was leading a life of dissipation and who owned a resort at which Pat and I frequently stayed. During those times many of the staff had come to know Jesus. The young man could see the change in the lives of those working for him, and obviously his heart began to hunger as God placed this hunger within him. Finally he approached me and told me that his life was empty. I was able to share my testimony with him. He listened avidly and, at the conclusion I asked him whether he would accept Jesus as his Lord and Saviour. This young man had been brought up in a Christian church but had given up his faith during his teenage life. He looked at me with great sorrow and said that he just could not give up the type of life he was now living. He began to weep.

I left him in his sorrow, thinking of the rich young ruler who went away sorrowing because he could not pay the price of following Jesus. However, the seed was sown, and the young man evidently decided to attend church, so every Sunday night he went to the local Anglican church. It was the start along the road to repentance. God knew his heart, and at the time of writing he is coming free of his old life; the demon powers are beginning to lose their grip upon him, and I have no doubt that he is close to true repentance and deliverance and that we will shortly see him as a completely renewed person in Jesus Christ.

Even when we are in the midst of battle, torn between our carnal desires and our desire to know the Lord, we only need to put our hand out towards Him and, if our heart is really open, then He can enter and begin to become Lord of our life.

However, it is vital that we exercise the will which God has given us and decide to follow Jesus as our Lord and Saviour so that our deliverance can be complete.

TWENTY FIVE

Keeping Our Deliverance

You never find flies around a place which is fully disinfected and clean. They hate the disinfectant.

In the case of the person who wants to retain their deliverance, they should always have the "disinfectant" of the Holy Spirit around them.

1. THE FIRST PRINCIPLE IS TO WALK IN THE SPIRIT.

This means leading a clean Holy life before God bringing every thought into captivity to Jesus Christ having received the baptism of the Holy Spirit.

> "Casting down arguments and every high thing that exhaults itself against the knowlege of God, bringing every thought into captivity to the obedience of Christ." (2 Corinthians 10:5)

2. READ THE WORD OF GOD DAILY.

There should be a balanced reading from the

scriptures each day. By "balanced" I mean read part of the Old Testament as well as part of the gospels and epistles. This does not need to be a lengthy reading; it should, however, be on a regular basis and on an ordered basis, so that there is a regular diet of the Word of God being fed to our spirit. The Word of God is the mirror of the Spirit and as we read the Word, we read about ourselves. All our faults are exposed in the mirror of God's Word and we are therefore able to deal with those faults. As we do so we are transformed by the power of the Word.

> *"But we all, with unveiled face, beholding as in a mirror the glory of the Lord, are being transformed into the same image from glory to glory, just as by the Spirit of the Lord."* (2 Corinthinans 3:18)

3. KEEP THE RIGHT COMPANY.

We are a separated people when we come to Jesus Christ, that is separated from the ways of the world. This does not mean to say that we should not move among the world and speak in love to those in the world, but in many cases we will need to keep away from the company of those who cause the problem, or who have the same problem. For example, if we are delivered from homosexuality, we must not go back amongst homosexuals, otherwise the weakness of our flesh will drag us back into the same problem again. Similarly, if we have been moving with a fast moving crowd and drinking, lusting, etc., we must break totally with fellowship from them. Some people decide to return and witness to those people, but in those circumstances we must be sure of our strength in the Lord before we attempt to do this. "Birds of a feather flock together", and if we again flock with the fast crowd, then we can expect real problems to arise.

"Do not be unequally yoked together with unbelievers. For what fellowship has righteousness with lawlessness? And what communion has light with darkness?

And what accord has Christ with Belial? Or what part has a believer with an unbeliever?" (2 Corinthians 6:14,15)

God then tells us to come out and be separate from them.

Therefore
"Come out from among them and be separate, says the Lord. do not touch what is unclean, and I will receive you." (2 Corinthians 6:17)

4. HAVE THE RIGHT FELLOWSHIP.

It is important that we fellowship in a Bible believing church and grow in things of the Holy Spirit. If our church appears to be "dead" simply because we have come to life, please remember the love that God still has for those in that particular church. Just because we have seen the light (it may have taken forty or fifty years for us to do so) do not expect everybody else to see the light within a few minutes. We may be called upon to show great love and tolerance towards those who are around us in that particular situation and continue to fellowship with them, so that they can see our changed life and desire to have the same. In such instances, I would counsel the person to stay in that situation but seek spiritual feeding, perhaps through a prayer group or anointed teaching in a church which appears to be "alive". In that way, our spiritual life can be fed and at the same time we can be witnesses to those who may be lost to God's great truths, to whom the Holy Spirit would dearly love us to minister in His love. Let us not be too quick to judge those who appear to be in a "dead" situation. Only God knows the heart of each person, and some apparently "dead" people spiritually often possess purer hearts and better attitudes than so many people who claim to be Spirit-filled believers.

In the same way, we are to fellowship in our daily life with those who are spirit filled, so that we can grow in God's grace and love.

> "And now abide faith, hope, love, these three; but the greatest of these is love" (1 Corinthians 13:13)

5. WE MUST BE CONTINOUSLY FILLED WITH THE HOLY SPIRIT.

> "And do not be drunk with wine, in which is dissipation; but be filled with the Spirit." (Eph. 5:18)

This means the fruit of the Holy Spirit should be evident in our lives: love, joy, peace, longsuffering, kindness, goodness, faithfulness, gentleness, self control (Galatians 5:22 & 23). If this fruit is operating in our lives, then there is little opportunity for the enemy to be active.

MAKE JESUS LORD AS WELL AS SAVIOUR OF OUR LIFE

Every part of our being needs to be yielded to the Lordship of Jesus Christ. There must be no secrets between us and Him. Our thought life, our physical life, our sexual life, and our emotional life, should be all under the Lordship of Jesus Christ and subject to Him.

"And whatever you do in word or deed, do all in the name of the Lord Jesus, giving thanks to God the Father through him" (Colossians 3:17).

If whatever we are doing gives glory to God, then we are safe.

JESUS SHOULD BE CENTRAL IN OUR LIFE

Jesus Christ should be the centre of our life during all our waking hours, so that we should be seeking to do things which are pleasing to Him. If this is so, then there will be little room for the devil to interfere.

"Looking unto Jesus, the author and finisher of our faith, who for the joy that was set before him endured the cross, despising the shame, and has sat down at the right hand of the throne of God." (Hebrew 12:2)

PUT ON THE WHOLE ARMOUR OF GOD

The word of God sets out our whole armour.

> "For we do not wrestle against flesh and blood, but against principalities, against powers, against the rulers of the darkness of this age, against spiritual hosts of wickedness in the heavenly places.
>
> Therefore take up the whole armour of God, that you may be able to withstand in the evil day, and having done all, to stand.
>
> Stand therefore, having girded your waist with truth, having put on the breastplate of righteousness,
>
> and having shod your feet with the preparation of the gospel of peace; above all, taking the shield of faith with which you will be able to quench all the fiery darts of the wicked one.
>
> And take the helmet of salvation, and the sword of the Spirit, which is the word of God;
>
> Praying always with all prayer and supplication in the Spirit, being watchful to this end with all perserverance and supplication for all the saints —" (Ephesians 6:12-18)

We should have our loins girded about with truth and put on the breastplate of righteousness and our feet shod with the preparation of the gospel of peace. Above all, we should take the shield of faith, whereby we can quench all the fiery darts of the wicked one, and the helmet of salvation which protects our mind. The sword of the Spirit, which is the Word of God, should always be in our hand, and finally we should be praying with all prayer and supplication in the Spirit.

The helmet of hope is the equivalent of the helmet of salvation.

We should always be open to praise God and take upon us the garment of praise.

"... *The garment of praise for the Spirit of heaviness"*. . . (Isaiah 61:3)

As we take on the garment of praise this keeps us free.

LOVING GOD

Finally we should aways remember to love the Lord our God with all our heart, with all our soul, with all our mind and with all our strength and to love our neighbour as ourselves.

Furthermore we should remember always to keep before us the new commandment that Jesus Christ gave us, namely to love one another as He loved us. If we are obedient to these commandments in all respects then our walk with the Lord will be a real and vibrant one and we will hold our deliverance.

TWENTY SIX

Teaching Through Groups

During recent times, I have found that people can be encouraged to know their authority in Jesus Christ by learning to operate in groups. I usually give a short teaching on the basic principles of deliverance, including describing demons and their manifestations, the requirements for deliverance and reasons why people are not delivered. I then break the session into groups of six or seven people and ask one person who believes that they have a problem to be a volunteer in the group.

When a person who has listened to the explanation about demon activity is aware that he may have a problem then he is encouraged to move forward in each group. Thus, with one person in each group desiring to become a candidate for deliverance, I then encourage the groups to take the person through the steps of repentance and renunciation of sin and then commence the forms of deliverance which we have given in chapter 17.

There is, however, one essential point before commencing this form of practice. I always encourage all the groups to invoke the power of the blood of Jesus and its protection over them.

The scriptures make it clear that we should have our senses exercised to discern good and evil:

"But solid food belongs to those who are of full age, that is, those who by reason of use have their senses exercised to discern both good and evil." (Hebrews 5:14)

We need to exercise the gifts that God desires to give us and as we "practise" this ministry as a group then various persons begin to operate in the gift of discernment.

Often a major manifestation begins, and I find as I move around all the groups, I am able to encourage each group in the methods of deliverance set out in Chapter (17). I make a particular point of encouraging any person who is manifesting to EXERCISE THEIR WILL. If they are making violent actions or noises, I tell them to exercise their will and be quiet as they have authority over the demon that is trying to work through them, and then as they appear to both exercise their will and repent, the person comes into deliverance.

We all need to be encouraged, and hence need to be equipped for the work of the ministry. We should be bold in our witness and in our expression of the love of Jesus Christ. In this way, we can indeed see the captives set free.

APPENDIX 1

Occult Check Sheet

Place a circle around any area which applies. Before proceeding, bind Satan and the Powers of Darkness and loose the person's mind to the Holy Spirit so that he can recall things that need to be remembered.

HAVE YOU BEEN INTO

Witchcraft, kabbala (occult lore), magic (not sleight of hand), blood subscriptions, hex signs, black magic (invoking hidden powers for bad ends), white magic (invoking hidden powers for good ends), hypnosis (whether magical or medical — it's dangerous), mental suggestion, mesmerism, self hypnosis (self-induced trance states), Gypsy curses put on you (death, injury, or calamity), Pk (parakineses — control of objects by the power of the mind and will), Tk (Telekinesis — objects move around the room, instruments play, engines start ...), black mass.

Do you carry an ankh (a cross with a ring top — used in satanic rites and dangerous).

HAVE YOU TAKEN PART WITH

ouija boards, planchette (glass on the table), seances, mediums, floating trumpets, disembodied voices etc., or consulted people who have clairvoyance (the ability to see objects or events spontaneously and supernormally beyond the natural range of vision —second sight), or clairaudience (ability to hear voices and sounds supernormally, spirited voices alleging to be that of dead people giving advice or warnings)?

HAVE YOU ENGAGED IN

activities involving mind reading, ESP (extra sensory perception), mental telepathy, thought transference, dream interpretation (as with the Edgar Cayce book)? or eckenkar or mind dynamics (Silva Mind Control) or touch for health.

HAVE YOU BEEN INTO

fortune telling by palm reading, tea leaf readings, phrenology (reading character, or one's future, by the conformations of a person's skull), crystal ball, cartomancy (using playing cards), tarot cards (22 picture cards for fortune telling), handwriting anaylsis, numerology (reducing the letters of one's name to numbers), astrology and horoscopes, psychometry (telling fortunes by lifting or holding object belonging to the enquirer), transcendental meditation.

HAVE YOU TRIED OR PRACTISED

divining, dowsing, or witching for water, minerals, underground cables, or finding out the sex of an unborn child using a divining rod, pendulum, twig or planchette. Also, the use of the pendulum, divining rod or a mechanical pendulum called a motor skopua for diagnosing illness and its treatment by colour therapy (using coloured threads) and "screening" (using copper coils etc)?

HAVE YOU SOUGHT

healings through magic practices using charms and charming for wart removal, death magic, (where the name of the sickness plus a written spell is cast into coffin or grave), acupuncture, acupressure, conjuration (summoning up a spirit by incantation), psychic healing, psychic surgery, concept therapy, or the use of a trance condition, or clairsentience (supernatural sense perception), or iridology (eye diagnosis to diagnose illnesses), sonarpuncture, radionics, astrologic medicine, chromotherapy, sound therapy, orgonomy.

HAVE YOU PARTICIPATED IN

levitation (body lifting by demonic power), table tipping, spirit knockings, rappings, or automatic (spirit) writing, Hallowe'en Parties?

HAVE YOU BEEN INVOLVED IN

yoga (exercises and meditation), karate, kung-fu,

aikido judo (martial arts), out-of-the-body (astral) travel of the soul?

HAVE YOU BEEN

trusting in amulets (tigers claw, sharks tooth, horse shoe over the door, mascots, gold earing (man), talisman (magic picture), letters (occult) of protection, zodiac charms (birthdates)) to compensate for lack of faith in God? Pagan fetishes (objects charged with magical powers and carried about as a means of protection or luck) come in the same category. Pagan religious objects, relics and artifacts which have been used in pagan temples or (pagan) religious rites, can be unknown to the owner, a focal point for evil influences in one's home, and should be burned.

Omens, significant days, moon-mancy, chain letters, and numerical symbolism and so on, exercise an occult superstitious bondage over many lives and should be dealt with.

HAVE YOU BEEN ON

Hallucinogenic drugs (LSD, heroin, marijuana etc) or sniffing thinners etc?

HAVE YOU BEEN INTO

heavy acid rock (e.g. Santana, Hendricks, Joplin, Deep Purple, Kiss, Black Sabbath etc) or in the Jonothan Livingstone Seagull sound track cult. (Such records should be destroyed). Some paintings, posters, etc., done under hallucinogenic stimulus can be oppressive and evil.

HAVE YOU VISITED

pagan rites such as Voodoo (West Indies) Sing Sings (New Guinea) Corroborees (Aust. Aboriginals) Fire Walking (Fiji, India) Umbahda and Macumba (Brazil) etc. Also visits to shows by Uri Geller or Mathew Manning demonstrating psychic powers could be dangerous.

DO YOU POSSESS

Occult Literature? In particular such books as "The 6th and 7th Book of Moses", "The Book of Venus", "The Other Side", "The Greater World", the pseudo-Christian works of Jacob Lorber, and works by other authors like Edgar Cayce, Jean Dixon, Ruth Montgomery, Arthur Ford, Anton Le Vay, Dennis Wheatley, Eckhart, and Johann Greber. Such books should be burned, regardless of cost. (Acts 19:19)

Transference can take place through contact with a formerly occult involved corpse. Occult powers, oppressions, illnesses etc. have inadvertently been "picked up" through contact in this way. Have you had any such experience?

I Timothy 4:1 says

"Now the Spirit expressly says that in latter times some will depart from the faith, giving heed to deceiving spirits and doctrines of demons."

The following is a list of cults and non-Christian religions which fall into the above category:-

Jehovah's Witnesses (Dawn Bible Students), Mormons (Church of Jesus Christ of the latter day Saints), Herbert W. Armstrong (Worldwide Church of God), Children of God, The Unification Church, (Moonies, One World Crusade), Unitarian Church, Christadelphians, Freemasonary, Spiritualism, Scientology, Christian Science, Rangatuism, Religious Science, Anthrosophy, Theosophy, Rosecrucianism, Inner Peace Movement, Spiritual Frontiers Fellowship, Eastern Religions such as:- Hare Krishna, Transcendental Meditation, Gurus, Divine Light Mission, Buddhism, Hinduism, Islam, Shintoism, Confucianism, Japanese Flower Arranging (sun worship), Bahai.

The Blood Scriptures

Eph. 1:7

"In him we have redemption through his blood, the forgiveness of sins, according to the riches of his grace."

Ps. 107:2

"Let the redeemed of the Lord say so, whom he has redeemed from the hand of the enemy:"

Therefore I can say:

THROUGH THE BLOOD OF JESUS I AM REDEEMED OUT OF THE HAND OF THE DEVIL. THROUGH THE BLOOD OF JESUS ALL MY SINS ARE FORGIVEN.

Rom. 5:9

"Much more then, having now been justified by his blood, we shall be saved from wrath through him."

Therefore I can say:

THROUGH THE BLOOD OF JESUS I AM JUSTIFIED, MADE RIGHTEOUS, JUST AS THOUGH I HAD NEVER SINNED.

    Heb. 13:12

"*Therefore Jesus also, that he might sanctify the people with his own blood, suffered outside the gate.*"

Therefore I can say:

THROUGH THE BLOOD OF JESUS I AM SANCTIFIED, MADE HOLY, SET APART TO GOD.

    1 Cor. 6:19,20

"Or do you not know that your body is the temple of the Holy Spirit who is in you, whom you have from God, and you are not your own?

For you were bought at a price; therefore glorify God in your body and in your spirit, which are God's."

    Rev. 12:11

"And they overcame him by the blood of the Lamb and by the word of their testimony, and they did not love their lives to the death."

Therefore I can say:

MY BODY IS A TEMPLE OF THE HOLY SPIRIT.

    I AM REDEEMED, CLEANSED, SANCTIFIED BY THE BLOOD OF JESUS, THEREFORE THE DEVIL HAS NO MORE PLACE IN ME AND NO MORE POWER OVER ME.

    THROUGH THE BLOOD OF JESUS I OVERCOME SATAN BY THE BLOOD OF THE LAMB AND THE WORD OF MY TESTIMONY.

Index